3000 800013 64513
St. Louis Community College

W9-DEE-309

FV

 St. Louis Community College

Library

5801 Wilson Avenue
St. Louis, Missouri 63110

Five Black Scholars
An Analysis of Family Life,
Education, and Career

FIVE BLACK SCHOLARS

An Analysis of Family Life, Education, and Career

Charles V. Willie

UNIVERSITY
PRESS OF
AMERICA

LANHAM • NEW YORK • LONDON

LIBRARY
ST. LOUIS COMMUNITY COLLEGE
AT FLORISSANT VALLEY

Abt
Books

Copyright © 1986 by

Abt Books

University Press of America,® Inc.

4720 Boston Way
Lanham, MD 20706

3 Henrietta Street
London WC2E 8LU England

All rights reserved

Printed in the United States of America

Co-published by arrangement with Abt Books

Library of Congress Cataloging in Publication Data

Willie, Charles Vert, 1927-
Five Black scholars.

Bibliography: p.
Includes index.
1. Afro-American scholars.   I. Title.
E185.96.W63   1986   305.8'96073   86-1663
ISBN 0-8191-5275-7 (alk. paper)
ISBN 0-8191-5276-5 (pbk. : alk. paper)

All University Press of America books are produced on acid-free
paper which exceeds the minimum standards set by the National
Historical Publications and Records Commission.

Contents

List of Tables

Preface

STUDIES OF RACIAL AND ETHNIC MINORITIES usually are designed as studies of social problems. Racial and ethnic groups are analyzed to determine how and why they deviate from the norm.

This study deliberately was designed to turn this custom around. The goal was to discover excellent black scholars in the social sciences and the humanities in the United States and to determine how they achieved eminence.

Although scholarly excellence among blacks and whites may be similar, the process of attainment could differ for minority and majority populations as a result of their unequal access to power and other resources; the fact that one group is dominant and the other subdominant in terms of power and authority relationships could make a difference.

The preferred research approach would be a study design that would facilitate a comprehensive and comparative analysis of black and white scholars. But resources were insufficient for such an analysis. Thus only case studies of black scholars were prepared because little is known about the developmental process in blacks of high achievement.

A reputational approach was used to identify outstanding scholars. A sample of the members of five professional associations was asked to rate black scholars who had been nominated as excellent representatives of their respective fields. One danger in using this approach is that creative people often stand alone, not with the crowd. In the end, however, their work must be vindicated by others who benefit from it. Reputational analysis as a way of identifying outstanding scholars is risky because it depends totally on the opinions of other professionals in a field. The risk of error in judgment, however, is probably less than that for a single researcher's opinion or for that of a small panel because a distorted judgment in a large population is diluted. The life histories of the five scholars selected attest to the validity of the reputational approach in identifying great scholars.

All studies in race are delicate, sometimes dangerous adventures. From whose point of view should data be interpreted—that of the minority or that of the majority? Judgments from both groups are used in this study—from professionals who identify with both minority and majority groups. The outstanding scholars included in this study were identified as outstanding by all.

This book is a study in the stages of adult development with special emphasis on humanistic and social science scholars. It focuses on the unfolding careers of successful people and identifies the decisive events in their lives. It is a study in human development that embraces social psychology, sociology, and ethnography.

Also presented is an analysis of the structural supports that sustain the professional careers of scholars, with particular attention to the function of family and education in career development. This book, then, is a study of social institutions and their interrelationship as manifested in the lives of professional scholars. These data reveal principles pertaining to social institutions and to the sociology of the professions.

The information contained in this book should be of practical benefit to young scholars who are in the process of building their careers and of theoretical value to research in sociology, psychology, and anthropology; and in the broader areas of race relations, human development, and higher education.

Acknowledged with special appreciation are the contributions to this study of Elfred Anthony Pinkard, Katharine O. Parker, and Elizabeth Blake. Research assistance was rendered by Anthony Pinkard, a candidate for the doctoral degree in education. Katharine O. Parker provided expert editorial assistance, and Elizabeth Blake was project secretary.

I personally interviewed the five outstanding scholars. I prepared case studies from information derived from the interviews, reviews of published materials, and conversations with the spouses of three of the scholars. These five scholars—Kenneth B. Clark; John Hope Franklin; Matthew Holden, Jr.; W. Arthur Lewis; and Darwin T. Turner—were generous with their time and graciously assisted by reviewing for errors, if any, material included in their biographical chapters. Nevertheless, I assume full responsibility for the focus of the biographies, including aspects of each scholar's professional career, family life, and formal education that are emphasized and significant events that have been omitted. Without the cooperation of the five scholars in revealing the details of their unfolding careers, this book could not have been written. All glory and honor to them for their unselfish ways and also to Mamie Clark, Gladys Isabel

Lewis, and Maggie Jean Turner, who provided additional information about the way of life of their spouses.

I also acknowledge with grateful appreciation the National Institute of Education (NIE) for supporting this study of "Characteristics That Contribute to Excellence among Black Scholars" through a grant (NIE-G-80-0035). Dr. Antoine Garibaldi provided helpful oversight as NIE project officer. The findings of this study do not necessarily reflect the position of the funding agency, and no official endorsement of these materials should be inferred.

October 1982
Harvard University
Cambridge, Massachusetts

CHAPTER 1

Life History as a Method of Investigation

IN HIS BOOK *Explorations in Social Theory*, William Goode states that "for nearly half a century, sociologists have paid little attention to historical data" (1973, p. 25). An increasing number of papers that are published in sociology journals "utilize data from one time point only" (Goode 1973, P. 25). Yet more and more historical studies are stimulated by sociological theory in that some now deal with ordinary social behavior, the main data of sociologists. Many sociologists, however, seem to be unaware of this fact (Goode 1973, p. 25). The social historians who try to account for and understand patterns of collective behavior acknowledge that "the concepts and procedures employed commonly come from adjacent social sciences" (Landes and Tilly 1971, p. 72).

Social historians, for example, are beginning to focus on what some have called *collective history*. This type of history analyzes, among other concerns, the biographies of political elites, patterns of social mobility, and major events in the past such as epidemics by examining systematically accumulated records of individuals (Landes and Tilly 1971, pp. 71–72). A salient characteristic of social history "is its extensive reliance on comparison . . . —the systematic, standardized analysis of similar social processes or phenomena . . . in different settings in order to develop and test general ideas of how those processes or phenomena work" (Landes and Tilly 1971, p. 73). The leaders of the discipline admit that comparative history "has

1

received a powerful impetus from the growing attention of historians to the generalizations of social and behavioral science;" they conclude that "history has as much to give to the other social sciences as they have to give to history" (Landes and Tilly 1971, pp. 72, 73).

The perspective of historians is beneficial in sociological analysis like that undertaken in this book because many historians may be classified as both humanists and social scientists. The humanists insist that human experience is best understood within the matrix of time and place. They believe that to extract human experience from its matrix is "an insult to the integrity of the historical process" (Landes and Tilly 1971, p. 10).

The purpose of this study is to determine the matrix of the lives of specific scholars and how it has contributed to their success. The scholars selected for study are blacks who work in the United States. Blacks are identified as the universe of study because of the paucity of our knowledge about their career patterns.

The methods of history and sociology are used in this investigation. A combination of general biographical facts and data derived from interviews about the family, educational, and career life histories of five outstanding black scholars was obtained. This information was assembled for individuals who were ranked as outstanding by a random sample of minority and of majority persons in their professional associations. The social sciences and humanities are appropriate fields to study. Toward the end of the 1970s, black scholars obtained doctoral degrees in education, the social sciences, and the humanities, in that order (*New York Times*, April 20, 1980: Educ 25), more than in other fields.

Officers and members of the governing boards of each of the major professional associations and of the most prominent black professional organizations were asked to nominate the three most outstanding black scholars in their respective fields. When it was not possible to obtain the membership lists of the governing boards of the black professional organizations, committees representing blacks within the major professional associations, or editorial boards of journals dealing with black cultural aspects of the fields, were surveyed. Thus, in addition to nominations from leaders in the American Economics Association, the American Historical Association, the American Philosophical Association, the American Psychological Association, the American Political Science Association, and the Modern Language Association, nominations were also obtained from leaders in the National Association of Black Economists, the editorial board of the *Journal of Negro History*, the Committee on the Status of Blacks in Philosophy, the editorial board of the *Journal of Black Psychology*, the National Conference of Black Political Scientists, and the College Language Association. The last six organizations are concerned largely with aspects of their discipline having to do with blacks.

The nominations from these sources were then tallied, and the scholars mentioned most frequently were listed as the panel of outstanding black scholars. In most cases it was possible to select the top three scholars in a field, but in some fields several scholars were tied for third place. Where there were ties, those tied were all listed as nominees.

The nominees had been selected by leaders in each field; but in order to obtain a broader representation of opinion concerning scholarly excellence, a sample of members of each field was asked to rank the nominees. One goal of the study was to obtain responses from members of the majority race as well as from members of minority groups. Therefore, the memberships of both the major national professional organization in each field and the national black professional organization in each field were sampled.

A random sample of members listed in the major national professional associations was selected. Two hundred names of nonstudent members of each major professional association were systematically drawn from the membership directories of each of the associations. The membership list of the College Language Association was obtained, and all members in the field of English were surveyed. The entire membership of the National Association of Black Economists was also surveyed.

In history, where the membership list of the Association for the Study of Afro-American Life and History was kept confidential, an arrangement was made with the custodian of the membership list to mail out the questionnaire from his headquarters. In political science, the membership list of the black organization was not available, nor did the president agree to mail out the questionnaires. Philosophy had no list of black members and no separate black group. For these three fields catalogues of 118 predominantly black colleges and universities were obtained, and questionnaires were sent to a sample of faculty members in each field. Faculty members at these schools are not always black, but this method was used in an attempt to increase the response rates among black scholars in these fields.

In all, a total of 1,200 members of the major professional organizations, 865 members of the black organizations, and the faculties of 118 predominantly black colleges and universities were sent ranking forms and questionnaires. The respondents were asked to rank the black scholars who had been nominated. They were also given the option of naming an excellent black scholar of their own choice who had not been nominated. Finally, respondents were asked to explain their reasons for their selections.

Many members of both majority and minority populations are reluctant to participate in surveys. The analysis of those who refused to participate is presented to indicate issues that should be considered in planning future investigations. Some, of course, refused to participate in the study and simply failed to acknowledge receipt of the letter.

Several nonrespondents claimed that the study was a waste of public resources, was not relevant to them particularly, or used a questionable data-gathering methodology. A few informants asked what would be done with the data. In other words, they wanted to know what policy implications could be drawn from the data, who would draw these implications, and how these implications would be applied in the development of public policy.

A few nonrespondents felt that the study was racist, since in their view scholarly excellence is the same for all racial groups. One respondent wrote, "the idea of this survey goes against the grain—it seems to permit the worst kind of racial stereotyping and I deeply regret that."

Some negative comments focused on the letter requesting cooperation in rating the nominated scholars. The covering letter stated that the life history of the ranking scholar would be useful as a role model. Individuals questioned whether the study could identify the best role model, and even the need for such an approach. One respondent stated, "I don't agree that your proposed life-history will be of obvious value; why should it be of any more value than role-models such as Curie, Galileo, or Archimedes?"

A few respondents and nonrespondents alike objected to the absence of women on the nomination list of outstanding scholars. In clarifying this concern, one respondent wrote, "I would also, as a woman, find it disheartening if you would give no consideration to providing a profile of women." Another wrote, "no book on Black scholars should be written without the inclusion of Black women. Blacks cannot afford to be either 'sexist' or 'racist.'" (It should be noted that the list of nominees was derived from knowledgeable scholars in each field and could not be controlled by the research staff.) These intense feelings about the absence of women indicates the extent to which women resent being unrecognized for their professional contributions.

Ten individuals offered methodological objections to the study. These included concern about the absence of objective criteria of scholarly excellence, and dissatisfaction with the nominating and ranking procedures for determining outstanding black scholars.

Participants in the study were asked to rank the individuals if they knew of their work, even if they did not know them personally; respondents were asked to rank such persons in terms of their own standards of scholarly excellence. Different individuals consider different contributions of a professional to be more or less significant in a particular field. By permitting each respondent to weight the characteristics that he or she considered more important, we were able to derive a range of definitions of excellence. Some respondents would have preferred that characteristics of scholarly excellence be specified so that they could rank the scholars nominated according to the predetermined characteristics; this approach was not used in this study.

Extraordinary efforts are needed to generate trust so that the public will participate in studies like this one. Race-relations research differs from other behavioral-science investigations in this respect. One way to accommodate the unique requirements of race-related studies is to provide sufficient resources to facilitate face-to-face interaction when possible in data collection. This approach and others that nurture trust and cooperation are essential in data collection for such studies.

Initially we planned to interview six outstanding scholars, but we reduced the number to five. Philosophy was eliminated from the case study because too few blacks were in the field to permit a valid reputational analysis of the most outstanding scholar; most professionals in this field did not know the nominees well enough to rank them.

The author interviewed each of the outstanding scholars to obtain information about current household, family of orientation, and other relevant experiences. According to Paul Lazarsfeld, contemporary information should be supplemented by information on earlier phases of whatever is being studied (quoted in Landes and Tilly 1971, pp. 72–73). The interviews provided information about the past that contributed to our understanding of the scholars' current circumstances.

Specifically, the scholars were asked questions about family background and economic circumstances; community race-relations climate; parents' philosophy of education; experiences in school, college, and graduate education; and career development. The case studies were prepared and submitted to each of the scholars for comments.

One goal of this study was to gain an understanding of the significant events and their interconnections in the life histories of our scholars and in the process of social interaction between them and others in the society. In effect, the five scholars were ideal types.

Classification of social facts is a perennial problem in social science research. Max Weber suggested that the description of types of social phenomena could be a starting point. According to G. Duncan Mitchell, the analyst who uses this method of analysis seeks to determine the extent to which individuals and their social practices conform to or deviate from the ideal (Mitchell 1968, pp. 87–89). Having no operational definition of ideal black scholarship, we decided to develop one inductively by analyzing the life histories of people identified by others in their field as outstanding. We call the five outstanding black scholars ideal types because they are models of success in professional achievement and career development.

These scholars nominated by black, white, and other professionals are marginal people who are known both within and beyond their racial group. Identified as marginal are people with experience in majority and minority cultures who may rise above the two groups in which they participate or fall between them. Everett Stonequist wrote that "the marginal [person] is the key personality in the contact of cultures. It is in his [or her] mind that the cultures come together, conflict, and eventually work out some kind of mutual adjustment and interpenetration." Stonequist concluded that "the life-histories of marginal [people] offer the most significant material for the analysis of the cultural process as it springs from the contact of social groups" (Stonequist 1937, p. 222). The life histories of the five scholars are studied from this perspective.

The case method is a useful way to study social organization, as Samuel Stouffer, the methodologist, proved in his doctoral dissertation submitted to the University of Chicago decades ago. He advocated use of the case method not only because it can obtain results that are similar to those obtained in quantitative studies, but also because it "suggest[s] connecting links in processes which may elude the statistician" (Stouffer 1980, p. 11 of abstract).

We were particularly interested in our scholars' educational odyssey from childhood through adulthood, although we focused on college and graduate school. We studied their careers from initial professional appointments to current work. We obtained the scholars' own interpretations of the meaning of various events in their unfolding careers. We obtained information on how each scholar decided to go into his chosen field, his area or areas of specialization, and any impediments he might have faced in career development.

According to Floyd Allport, the life history of each scholar is a structure of ongoing events that is "self-limiting" and "unified." The whole is different from the separate parts; yet the whole is pervasive throughout all the parts so that a system can relate through events that which is "inside" to that which is "outside" and can link that which comes "before" to that which comes "after," that which is "below" to that which is "above" (Allport 1955, pp. 615–619).

Using the event-structure theoretical framework of Allport, we attempted to discover critical events in the life histories of the five scholars. We examined the stages in the life cycle, and the significant events that separated or linked these stages or ongoing processes. For example, we identified the age at which each scholar entered college, the number of years of matriculation before graduation, the age at which graduate study began, the length of time between the commencement and the end of graduate study, and professional employment before and after receipt of terminal degree. We determined the scholar's length of affiliation with various employers, including events of promotion or demotion, and the assumption of new and different roles and responsibilities. We examined the quantity and quality of professional publications, the age at which publishing began, the rate of publishing, and the receipt of professional honors and other recognitions.

Data on personal events were also obtained. These included information on age at marriage, date of marriage in relation to college graduation and graduate study, length of marriage, number of offspring, and age at birth of offspring.

Examining the structure of events in the ongoing education and career processes of each scholar enabled us to identify events that served as barriers or inducements to movement from one stage to another. It also allowed us to determine similarities, if any, in the pattern of structured events in the lives of our ideal-type scholars.

Our approach was similar to one employed in the medical educational pathway analysis. That study, concerned with efforts to achieve equal representation of minority students in medicine, identified the interrelated events in becoming a physician, such as becoming a qualified medical school applicant, becoming a medical school student, becoming a medical school graduate, becoming a licensed physician, and becoming a practicing physician. Linkages between processes were examined to determine what the researchers called *action elements* that encourage exit from the educational pathway or contribute to student retention (Health Resources Administration 1977, pp. 22–46).

The organization of information by ongoing processes (or stages or seasons) that are separated by significant events appeared to be a helpful way of studying the life histories of our scholars. Daniel Levinson and his collaborators discovered that "each phase in the life cycle has its own virtues and limitations. To realize its potential value, we must know and accept its terms and create our lives within it accordingly" (Levinson 1978, p.x). If one can identify what is done in various stages of the education and career-development process, and how it is done, such research discoveries may be of value to young scholars who are building a career.

To determine similarities and differences among the five scholars, a table was constructed that symbolically represented a family-education-career tree. The age at which the five scholars did or did not accomplish various things are the limbs of the tree. We consolidated the data for the separate scholars into a composite portrait of family, education, and career development.

These data gave a time and space perspective on family, education, and career development and the relationship between these ongoing processes and significant events. This approach, like the one used by Lewis Terman and Melita Oden in their logitudinal study of gifted people, enables us to determine not only what scholars do with gifts in mental ability, but also how and when they use their gifts (1960, pp. 823–833).

Of the 554 individuals in our nationwide sample of humanists and social scientists, 405 responded to our request to rank several scholars in their field who had been nominated as outstanding. Table

Table 1-1
Criteria of Outstanding Professional Status for Black Scholars in the Humanities and Social Sciences Reported by a National Sample of Professional Association Members, by Race

Criteria	Percentage				Rank				Ratio of Total Percentage to Race Percentage		
	Total N = 405	Black N = 152	White N = 222	Other N = 31	Total	Black	White	Other	Black	White	Other
Scholarship	46.4	51.3	42.3	51.6	1	1	1	1	1.10	.91	1.11
Professional association activity	7.6	7.2	7.7	10.0	2	4.5	2.5	3	.95	1.01	1.32
Public service	6.9	7.9	5.4	12.9	3	3	4	2	1.14	.78	1.87
Professional reputation	6.2	4.6	7.7	3.2	4	6	2.5	5.5	.74	1.24	.52
Competence	5.2	8.5	2.7	6.4	5	2	5.5	4	1.63	.52	1.23
Teaching	3.0	3.9	2.7	—	6.5	7	5.5	—	1.30	.90	—
Commitment to black community	3.0	7.2	.4	—	6.5	4.5	8.5	—	2.40	.13	—
Institutional affiliation	1.7	2.0	1.8	—	8	8	7	—	1.18	1.06	—
Integrity	.7	.7	.4	3.2	9	9	8.5	5.5	1.00	.57	4.57

1-1 presents a distribution by race of reasons for ranking a scholar; 55 percent of the reasons were offered by white respondents, 37 percent by black respondents, and 8 percent by respondents classified as other minorities. Some respondents ranked the nominated scholars but did not give reasons for their choices; others gave several reasons for ranking a scholar as outstanding. All tc ld, two-thirds of the respondents ranked the scholars and gave reasons they used to make their decisions.

A substantial proportion of all respondents listed scholarship as the main reason for classifying a scholar as outstanding. This category referred to research, writing, and publications. Each of the eight other reasons was subscribed to by less than one-tenth of all respondents.

Blacks and whites agreed that scholarship was the main indicator of outstanding professional status in the humanities and social sciences. In addition to scholarship, the other criteria used by all (in order of significance as determined by frequency of response) were professional association activity, public service, professional reputation, competence (including intelligence and creativity), teaching, commitment to the black community, institutional affiliation, and integrity (including honesty and objectivity). Some of these have to do with personal attributes and others with organizational participation.

The distributions of the reasons for ranking an individual as outstanding were analyzed by race. Although there is a positive correlation between the ranking system employed by the two racial populations there are some differences in definitions of outstanding professional status.

At the top and bottom of the distributions, there was agreement between blacks and whites that research, writing, and publishing (generically called *scholarship*) are important components of outstanding professional status, and also that integrity is important enough to be listed but least important in the nine-item hierarchy. After scholarship, blacks listed competence, public service, professional association activity, and commitment to the black community as most important in their hierarchy of criteria of outstanding professional status; these were in the top half of their hierarchy. Whites also identified scholarship as the main criterion, followed by professional association activity, professional reputation, and public service as the other criteria in the top half of their hierarchy. Black and white scholars disagreed on the relative importance of competence, professional reputation, and commitment to the black community; but they agreed with only minor differences on the significance and rank of scholarship, professional association activity or participation, and public service.

One could argue that the two categories, competence and professional reputation, are different indicators of the same phenomenon. Blacks prefer to assess intelligence and creativity directly as a personal attribute, which they call *competence*. Whites prefer to assess these indirectly as a reflection of *reputation*. If we assume that competence and professional reputation are merely two different indicators of intelligence and creativity, then the major difference between the races in their hierarchy of criteria is the inclusion of commitment to the black community in the top half of the hierarchy by blacks and the exclusion of this item in the top half by whites. If one classifies blacks' concern about commitment to the black community as self-serving, then one can understand why whites omitted such an item from the top half of their hierarchy of indicators.

A more philosophical issue arises with respect to what should and should not be included in a hierarchy of indicators of outstanding professional status. Observers of human nature and of social relations with very different perspectives—such as Neal Pierce, the journalist; Eric Hoffer, the longshoreman and writer; and Samuel Bowles and Herbert Gintis, the economists—have arrived at similar conclusions about the function of subdominant populations in the power structure for the total society. Pierce wrote "A society deserves to be judged on how it treats its least fortunate members" (1981, p. 14). In more colorful language, Hoffer called the subdominant people of power "the dregs" who, as they rise to the top, manifest the innermost worth of a nation (1963, p. 148). Bowles and Gintis set forth this principle: "The humanity of a nation, it is said, can be gauged by the character of its prisons" (1976, p. 102). All this suggests that a concern about subdominant populations may be a universal requirement of anyone who aspires to be outstanding.

According to the hierarchy of values expressed by blacks in our study, no one who is callous about oppression, indifferent or uncommitted to the people who experience it, can be considered an outstanding scholar in the humanities and the social sciences. Along with the criteria of research, writing, publishing, intelligence, creativity, public service, and professional association activity, blacks have added an ethical requirement of concern for the poor, oppressed, and afflicted for those who would be called outstanding. It could be that this indicator of outstanding professional status should be included as an important one by all groups. According to this analysis, professional achievement must be concerned with the advancement of the group as well as with self-enhancement.

There is cause for celebration that consensus exists between the racial populations regarding scholarship, professional association activity, and public service as important criteria of outstanding professional status. It is regrettable that teaching is ranked by all in the bottom half of the nine-item hierarchy. There is also cause for some consternation that both black and white scholars share the belief that integrity is of least importance among the criteria listed as an indicator of outstanding professional status.

It would have been fruitful if black women scholars had been included in the analysis. Some women were nominated, but none was rated the most outstanding in her field by the sample of raters. Considering the way a sexist society has distributed opportunities for professional advancement in the past, it would be appropriate to undertake a study of stages in the development of career, education, and family life of minority women, even as this book—though not fully anticipated or planned with this in mind—is a study of outstanding black men.

CHAPTER **2**

The Historian Who Understands

John Hope Franklin

IN HIS IMPORTANT STUDY *The Seasons of a Man's Life*, psychologist Daniel J. Levinson reviews the story of Faust and describes his quest for knowledge as the hubris of the scientist (Levinson 1978, p. 249). Philosopher Huston Smith, author of *Forgotten Truth*, goes one step further and classifies our hunt for knowledge of humanity as "the final exploitation" because of the built-in violence that reduces the object of knowledge to object (Smith 1976, p. 126). These consequences of knowledge-getting in the humanities and social sciences—self-serving glorification or destructive reductionism—can be prevented only if while getting knowledge one also seeks understanding. This is precisely what the historian, John Hope Franklin, has done.

In the history that Franklin writes, knowledge and understanding are complementary: One without the other is incomplete. His contribution has been to make history a field of wisdom, devoid of the cult of fictitious glorification of a whole society or the cant of quantitative reductionism that analyzes parts out of context.

By any measure, John Hope Franklin—for more than a decade the John Matthews Manly Distinguished Service Professor at the University of Chicago (Emeritus in 1982), and later James B. Duke Professor of History, Duke University—is one of the most celebrated historians in the United States. His book *From Slavery to Freedom*, now in its fifth edition, has been described as the best history of black Americans. Thrice honored by professional peers, Franklin has been elected president of three of the most prestigious historical organizations in the United States.

How could a black person born in Rentiesville, Oklahoma, a relatively poor, all-black town of approximately 200 (to which Franklin's family moved as a temporary protection against the outrage of discrimination) achieve so much so well, not exhibit the slightest trace of arrogance? His ability to remain unpretentious with his colleagues, accessible to his students, kind in his criticism, and generous in his praise is a significant aspect of the John Hope Franklin saga—as important as his scholarly achievements.

INFLUENCE ON THE FIELD OF HISTORY AND RECOGNITION BY PEERS

In the process of being truly generous to persons near and dear to him, Franklin has managed not only to write good history but also to make history through the development of his wide-ranging career as teacher, researcher, administrator, and policymaker. The listing of his works cited by other scholars in 1975 and 1976, for example, demonstrates his extensive influence on contemporary scholarship. The Social Science Citation Index reported that at least fifteen different books and articles by Franklin were cited in approximately fifty social science journals during this two-year period. His works were cited by scholars in a number of different disciplines. To illustrate, he was cited in *Social Work, Journal of Negro Education, Social Problems, Journal of Politics*, and *American Sociological Review*, to name a few, as well as several history journals. The most frequently cited reference was his basic text, *From Slavery to Freedom*; about one-third of all references had to do with material from that book, of which approximately 900,000 copies have been sold.

Franklin has continued to do good research and to function as a productive scholar. An important book, *Southern Odyssey*, won the Jules Landry Award from the Louisiana State University Press for the best manuscript submitted in 1975 in history, biography, or literature. Between 1943 and 1981 Franklin was author or editor of seventeen books, an average of about one book every two years.

Franklin is recognized by his peers of all races and in all regions as an excellent historian—the most outstanding black historian. This conclusion is based on our survey. Selected white and black scholars associated with advisory boards and governing councils of national professional and scholarly organizations in the field of history were each asked to nominate at least three outstanding black scholars.

John Hope Franklin was most frequently nominated by individuals in all racial populations. The names of the four scholars with multiple nominations were submitted as a panel to a national random sample of 109 professional historians, both black and white; they were asked to rank the panel of four in terms of their own criteria of scholarly excellence and to submit additional names if none in the panel met their criteria. Only one name was added by one of the 109 in the national sample. Ten returned the survey instrument and stated that they did not wish to participate in the study. Of the 99 professional historians who ranked the panel of five (which included four nominees and one added by a rater), 66 gave John Hope Franklin a first-place vote as the outstanding black scholar in history.

SCHOLARSHIP

Franklin's reputation clearly transcends racial boundaries. John Hope Franklin is a real scholar; and the real, as Huston Smith stated, always has a transcendent character (Smith 1976, p. 142). "I have said I was a mainstreamer," Franklin reports. "Even in my graduate work, I refused to get put over in a corner and made a stereotype." Before selecting his dissertation topic on the free Negro in North Carolina, Franklin went through several metamorphoses at Harvard. While matriculated as a graduate student, he published a paper on "Edward Bellamy and the Nationalist Movement" (Franklin 1938). He considered doing research on Christian Socialism and almost decided to specialize in British history. He pulled back from each of these topics for various reasons, however, and finally followed through with research on free Negroes, a project he had begun as an undergraduate student with his history teacher at Fisk University. His focus on the South and on blacks, in his opinion, are investigations concerned with "the mainstream." Franklin told Jack Star, who was preparing an article for *Change* magazine: "I don't teach black history at the University of Chicago. I teach the history of the South—black and white" (Star 1977, p. 28). His focus on the South is an effort to understand the condition of our total society.

The transcendent character of Franklin's scholarship is revealed in his analytical approach of "maintaining a discreet balance" and giving "proper consideration for anonymous as well as outstanding people" (Franklin 1977, p. xiv).

As a referee of the past, Franklin classifies events as they are, not as he or others would prefer that they be. When his book *The Militant South* was being considered for publication by the Harvard University Press, one Southern white historian questioned whether the manuscript should be published. Then the Southerner conceded that it might be all right to publish if a view of the South by a black was what the press wanted (Star 1977, p. 30). This evaluation illustrates the destructiveness of reductionism. To emphasize the race of the historian is to deny Franklin's skills in scholarly research. Franklin believes that "there are more valid standards by which to judge a people than race" (1960, p. 17). Fortunately, the Harvard University Press took a similar view and published the book.

Franklin's service as president of the Southern Historical Association was particularly significant in light of his criticism of some southern scholarship. In 1960, years before becoming the head of the Southern Historical Association, Franklin stated that "nowhere in the United States . . . has the cult of history flourished as it has flourished in the South" (1960, p. 17). He has been both criticized and praised for such candor.

Nevertheless, Franklin knew that "history has been an important instrument in shaping human affairs" (Franklin 1960, p. 17). He believed that a distorted historical tradition could be corrected and that a correct history could help change a churlish and shortsighted reaction to ongoing events in the South. Thus Franklin's honest assessments were made for the purpose of helping the South and ultimately the nation. The South, according to Franklin, "has been continuously both southern and American" (1960, p. 18).

FAMILY BACKGROUND

How did Franklin become the person he is? A look at his family background is instructive. First of all, Franklin comes from a professional family; he is not a first-generation college graduate. Franklin's father, originally from the Indian Territory, attended Morehouse College in Atlanta, Georgia, Roger Williams College (now defunct) in Nashville, Tennessee, and Kent College of Law for a brief time. John Hope Franklin was named in honor of the first black president of Morehouse College, John Hope.

Franklin's parents met at Roger Williams College, where his mother completed the normal school course of study for teachers. The family settled in Oklahoma, where Franklin's father passed the state bar, finishing second among all who took the examination. The family first lived in Ardmore, Oklahoma; then in Rentiesville, an all-black town; and finally in Tulsa. While Franklin's father practiced law, his mother (Mollie) taught elementary school in the periods between giving birth to four offspring, of whom John Hope Franklin was the youngest.

Franklin's father, infuriated by an incident of discrimination in the court, moved the family to the all-black town of Rentiesville to protect them against the type of insults he had experienced. Actually the incident occurred not in Oklahoma but in Shreveport Louisiana.

where Franklin's father had gone to represent a client. The judge there told him, "No nigger is going to represent any client in my court," and ordered him to sit down or get out.

While practicing law in Rentiesville, where a daughter and John Hope were born, the elder Franklin (Buck Colbert) was the postmaster and justice of the peace. The town, with only about 200 people, was too small to support a viable law practice.

John Hope Franklin remained in Rentiesville until he was ten years. When he was growing up, there was no day care for the children of working parents. Franklin's mother took him with her to the school in which she taught, had him sit on the back bench in her classes, and told him to be quiet: "I learned to read by sitting in on her classes." His mother was pleased to discover that he, though only a preschooler, was learning to read along with the school-age children. Franklin said that his mother had high expectations for all her children, and all the Franklin offspring finished high school and college.

When John Hope was only six, his father decided to risk the outside world again to establish a full-time law practice. He moved to Tulsa, coming home from time to time to visit his family. He surmised that by the end of that current school year his wife would be able to stop working so that the whole family could move to the city. Bad luck struck again, however. Six months after Franklin's father opened a law office in Tulsa, the 1921 race riot in that city wiped out everything and his father's office was burned to the ground. His father did not recover from his losses until 1925. Then, when Franklin, the youngest child, was ten, the family moved to Tulsa, and Franklin's mother retired from teaching.

Franklin was pleased to be with his father regularly again. Despite the bad experiences in Louisiana and initially in Tulsa, Franklin said that his father ignored segregation whenever he could. He recalled that as a child he went to court with his father and sat at the lawyer's table: "I learned to be an integrationist from my father."

Tulsa proved to be a more viable setting for a law practice, but the financial reverses associated with the 1921 riot had strained household funds. The family could muster college tuition, but postgraduate education payments were beyond their means.

EDUCATION

High School

Franklin described his high school years in Tulsa as normal. They occurred during the age of segregation, when by law blacks and whites were assigned to different schools. His teachers were good:

"They gave me a sense of self-confidence." In high school, Franklin also learned to type and take shorthand, skills that helped finance college and graduate school. The class valedictorian, Franklin graduated from high school in Tulsa at the age of sixteen.

College

Franklin left Oklahoma and traveled to Nashville, Tennessee, to enroll in Fisk University. His parents knew that Nashville was an educational center, having studied there earlier. His brother had gone to Fisk. Always ready to rise to any challenge, Franklin said: "I figured I could do anything my brother could do. So I went to Fisk, intending to be a lawyer."

Franklin's career plans changed abruptly during his sophomore year: "At Fisk, I met a young professor, a young white professor, born in Amesbury, Massachusetts. He was a historian and specialized in Latin American history. This young professor was named Theodore S. Currier. He was a person with great charm and became my mentor. I took a course with Theodore Currier. He discovered that I had some promise, and he nurtured me to attend Harvard. Currier taught American history to me my second year in college. I had never had such an intellectual experience."

After taking more history courses, Franklin said, he understood what a historian was and that he wanted to be one. He enjoys trying to understand the present by looking at the past, "putting things together with small clues." Other experiences at Fisk, where Franklin was secretary to the librarian, were helpful also. He said that the education and support he received in college were so effective that he was not awed by graduate school.

Graduating magna cum laude from Fisk at the age of twenty, Franklin applied to and was accepted for graduate study by Harvard University. When Franklin reached his senior college year, Currier had advised him to go to Harvard to study history. But the year was 1935, in the middle of the Depression. Despite his aspirations, Franklin understood his family's financial situation: "My father's law business had been crushed by the Depression, so the family could not finance my graduate study." Returning home the summer after graduating from college, Franklin wondered what to do.

When Currier heard of Franklin's problems, he said, "Money will not keep you from going to Harvard!" He asked if Franklin could make it to Nashville, where the two might try to find a solution. There was no source they could tap for funds. So Currier, a thirty-three-year-old professor who had joined the Fisk faculty in 1929, went to the bank and borrowed enough money to pay for Franklin's first year at Harvard.

Currier helped John Hope Franklin and many more students like him. Several outstanding blacks—such as the historian L. D. Reddick who prepared a biography of Martin Luther King, Jr., and the Montgomery bus boycott, and the lawyer Wade McCree, former solicitor general of the United States—were taught by Currier and graduated from Fisk. It was, in part, through Currier's efforts that a chapter of Phi Beta Kappa was established at Fisk, with John Hope Franklin as a founding member. Currier remained on the Fisk faculty more than forty years; he died in 1979.

Franklin is the executor of Currier's estate, and he and his wife are setting up a scholarship at Fisk in Currier's honor. The Franklins are contributing to it and will turn over the proceeds from the sale of Currier's estate to the fund: "We hope it will become the largest scholarship fund at Fisk." Hearing Franklin reminisce about his relationship with Currier, one can understand why he would like to perpetuate the name of his mentor: "Currier was my closest friend. We started out in a student-teacher relationship but became very close friends. He had a forty acre place in Maine that I visited often during the summer months." Franklin will always remember Currier's decisive statement: "Money will not keep you from going to Harvard!"

Graduate School

At Harvard, Franklin first studied for the M.A. degree in history which he earned in one year. He financed the first stage of his graduate education with the bank loan that Currier made, small contributions from his father, and with earnings as dishwasher and typist.

After teaching a year at Fisk, Franklin returned to Harvard in 1937 to receive the Ph.D. degree in history, which he received in 1941 at the age of twenty-six, just six years after his college graduation. This was remarkably quick in view of the fact that his studies were twice interrupted by full-time teaching assignments—first at Fisk for one year, then at St. Augustine's College in North Carolina for the first two of the total of four years he taught there.

While teaching at St. Augustine's, Franklin, who had completed the residency requirement for the Ph.D. degree between 1937 and 1939, did research for his dissertation, "The Free Negro in North Carolina, 1790–1860." In 1943, two years after his Ph.D. degree was awarded, Franklin's dissertation was published by the University of North Carolina Press.

Franklin did so well at Harvard in his first year of matriculation that several opportunities came his way in subsequent years. When he returned to Harvard to study for the Ph.D. degree, he was "loaded" with scholarship assistance. In general, he said, "I experienced no serious impediment at Harvard." He believes that the level of sensitivity of the university has increased over the years. "It definitely was not immune from racism when I was there," he observed; but "I decided that if Harvard let us in the door, that was enough. I would take it from there. So I experienced no serious impediments." For Franklin the young scholar, Harvard was "a tremendous experience."

As stated before, Franklin attributed his capacity to deal with Harvard without awe to the self-confidence he had developed in high school and the education and support he received in college. In essence, Franklin's Harvard education was successful because of his Tulsa, Oklahoma, and Nashville, Tennessee experiences.

CAREER

Stage I

Franklin's professional career proceeded as smoothly as his education. Franklin spent a year at his alma mater as an instructor after receiving his M.A. degree. His first real professional appointment and the beginning of his career as a professional historian was at St. Augustine's College in Raleigh, North Carolina, in 1939. Although his Ph.D. degree had not yet been awarded, Franklin was hired at St. Augustine's as a professor because rank meant very little there. Thus Franklin, though only twenty-four-years-old, began his academic career at the highest academic rank. St. Augustine's, of course, was not as competitive as some of the schools where he later would teach. Franklin remained there four years and then moved on for another four years at North Carolina College, a predominantly black state-supported institution in Durham, North Carolina. Then, at thirty-two, he went to Howard University in Washington, D.C., as professor of history.

Stage II

During his nine years at Howard University, Franklin's career as a historian flourished. In 1947, the year he moved to Washington, D.C., the first edition of his most widely ready book, *From Slavery to Freedom*, was published by Alfred A. Knopf. In this period, also, he completed research on his own favorite of his books, *The Militant South*. These were the years when Franklin and other social scientists made history by contributing their research skills to the preparation of the case that resulted in the 1954 U.S. Supreme Court opinion in *Brown* v. *Board of Education* that outlawed segregation in public education.

Franklin is most pleased about his participation in the preparation of the school-desegregation court case. First, he found action compatible with his own inclination toward the mainstream. Second, he sees no conflict between scholarship and action in public affairs, which he regards as "a way of enhancing and deepening one's understanding of what is going on." For three months, while teaching at Howard, Franklin devoted about four days a week to the *Brown* case. His specific responsibility was to research the debates and circumstances associated with the passage of the Fourteenth Amendment to the U.S. Constitution. The Court wanted to know if the framers of the amendment understood that the Court could construe the amendment as abolishing segregation. Franklin assesses the *Brown* effort as "one of the best examples of historians influencing public policy."

Franklin justifies his involvement in public policymaking as a survival stratagem. To survive as a scholar, he said, he must also survive as a man—as a black man. Franklin believes that the black scholar must perform a dual role—practicing scholarship that adheres to the highest standards in the field, and advocating justice and equality. This dual approach will enable the black academician "to be heard as a scholar and to survive as a human being." Motivated by this philosophy, John Hope Franklin has been ceaselessly involved in public affairs.

Franklin described his time in Washington as "the golden years of Howard." He was experiencing comprehensive development both as a professional scholar and as a man of public affairs. He associated with a variety of exciting people at Howard University— the historian Rayford Logan, the sociologist E. Franklin Frazier, the specialist in English, Sterling Brown, and the philosopher Alain. Locke. "Yet," Franklin said, "there was something that was not quite right at that time."

The "something" was the fact that Franklin's professional opportunities were restricted largely to segregated settings. All four schools in which he had taught were predominantly black. He specialized in the history of the South, but as late as 1948 no black historian had been recognized as worthy of presenting a professional paper at the annual meetings of the Southern Historical Association. In 1956 a white historian expressed doubts about the value of Franklin's manuscript on *The Militant South* because of the author's race, and questioned whether the book, which was later widely and favorably reviewed, should even be published. Segregation was an impediment to anyone who wished to be part of the mainstream.

As mentioned earlier, Franklin was always ready to respond to a challenge. He did this by breaking the color line that W. E. B. DuBois had forecast as "the problem of the twentieth century" (DuBois 1903). In 1949 Franklin became the first black historian to read a paper before the Southern Historical Association. Together with lawyers and other social scientists, he destroyed legal sanctions for racial segregation in public education in the *Brown* v. *Board of Education* case of 1954. By 1956 Franklin was ready to break the color line against the employment of black historians in high-level positions at predominantly white colleges and universities.

Stage III

As a continuation of his effort to be part of the mainstream, Franklin accepted an invitation to come to Brooklyn College in New York City as professor and chairman of the Department of History.

Franklin visualized this offer as a new opportunity to contribute to the field of history. In addition to writing and doing research at Brooklyn, he took on the challenge of uniting a split department: "I quelled arguments and was able to smooth out the problems." Serving for eight years as chairman of the history department, Franklin described his Brooklyn experience as "a marvelous time."

After twenty-five years of solid work as a scholar, which included the writing of six books, the editing of four others, and the preparation of more than twenty-one articles and chapters in books, Franklin's reputation began to soar as he turned fifty. In addition to his publications, many people knew of Franklin because of the many papers he had read at meetings of professional associations.

Stage IV

Now the University of Chicago sought Franklin's services. The twentieth century was nearly two-thirds spent; yet Franklin, a scholar of note, had not been recruited for a permanent appointment by any of the most distinguished history departments in the United States. The University of Chicago launched a campaign to rectify this omission and to attract Franklin to its campus. Franklin had been offered appointments at other prestigious universities, but not in his field. The University of Chicago, however, understood the significance of Franklin's unique contribution as an authority on the history of the South. It was able to understand and make a proper assessment of Franklin's talents, probably, because it "had the oldest chair in southern history outside the South" (Star 1977, p.29). The University of Chicago sent an emissary to Europe, where Franklin was on leave from Brooklyn, to determine his possible response to an invitation to join its faculty.

Franklin informed the emissary that he intended to continue his scholarly career and had rejected opportunities for ambassadorial and other public-service appointments. Whether he would consider an invitation to join the faculty of the University of Chicago was something he would have to decide when the actual invitation was extended. Sensing that Franklin might respond favorably and wishing to obtain a commitment before others might approach him, the University of Chicago offered John Hope Franklin a tenured professorship even before he visited the campus. Five years later it named him the first John Matthews Manly Distinguished Service Professor of History. With the ebullience characteristic of his esponse to all his professional opportunities, Franklin called his sixteen years at the University of Chicago (three of which were served as chairman of the Department of History) "a most satisfying intellectual experience." Retiring from the University of Chicago in 1982, he retains the rank of emeritus professor.

John Hope Franklin had to initiate his scholarly activities, but subsequent career promotions were initiated by others. He preferred that his career unfold this way: "I have never been the kind of person who schemes and plans his moves, who plans to be at one place now and then at another later."

PUBLIC AND PROFESSIONAL HONORS

In his younger years Franklin was generous in his praise of others, especially those who worked for and with him. In his mature years, others have heaped praises on him. In almost every year beyond his fiftieth birthday, a new honor has come Franklin's way. For example, at the age of fifty-two, Franklin was president of the American Studies Association; at fifty-six, president of the Southern Historical Association. The United Chapters of Phi Beta Kappa installed him as president the year he turned 58. He served as president of the Organization of American Historians when he was fifty-nine; finally, at sixty-four he was elected to the presidency of the American Historical Association.

Beyond these professional honors, Franklin was inducted into the Oklahoma Hall of Fame when he was sixty-three years old and was given an honorary degree by Harvard University in 1981 when he was sixty-six, forty years after he earned a Ph.D. degree from that school.

John Hope Franklin is the kind of person who can come home again. He returned to the city of his youth to receive an honorary degree from the University of Tulsa. He returned to each of the universities from which he graduated—Fisk and Harvard—to receive an honorary degree. He returned to two of the schools at which he was a former faculty member—Howard and Brooklyn—to receive honorary degrees. All told, he has been so honored by more than seventy colleges and universities in the United States and by Cambridge University in England. (The Cambridge honor is amusing in that Franklin, who flirted with the idea of specializing in British history while he was in graduate school, decided against it because he thought that he never would be able to visit that country.)

PERSONAL CHARACTERISTICS

John Hope Franklin is a cosmopolitan person. He has visited England, the USSR, China, Japan, and India; several countries in Africa; and others in Europe, Asia, and elsewhere.

John Hope Franklin's public life and private life are coordinated and unified so that each is supported and sustained by the other. His best-selling book *From Slavery to Freedom* is dedicated to his wife, Aurelia, whom he married in 1940 when he was twenty-five, after he had completed his residency requirements for the Ph.D. degree at Harvard and one year before the degree was awarded.

Others have put their trust in John Hope Franklin, and Franklin has put his trust in his wife. He said, "She always has had a good feeling about what was happening to me and knew what was appropriate." Married more than forty years, Franklin values his wife's advice on professional as well as on personal matters. The two met at Fisk and have been "going together since college days." Reflecting on their union and its meaning for his career, Franklin said emphatically, "I know my life would not have been as stable personally as it has been, if it had not been for my wife."

The Franklins have one son, a graduate of Stanford University, who is adept at languages and fluent in French. He has lived in Africa for several years and has taught English as a foreign language in Dakar, Senegal.

In addition to his warm and sustaining family, Franklin supports a life of productive scholarship with, in his words, "an enormous amount of energy." He acknowledges that he is tenacious and that he labors to overcome obstacles: "I can work longer and harder than most people. My work day is very long." Equally important, Franklin is enthusiastic about what he does. His recreational interest are varied. He pursues a vigorous program of exercise and diet and cultivates 500 rare orchids, a bloom from one of which is usually exhibited in his lapel (Star 1975, p. 33).

Franklin is a man of many interests, manifested in his private and public lives. His reader on the struggle for civil rights, for example, includes cartoons, speeches, statistics, excerpts from state laws, other documents, and the results of public-opinion polls (Franklin and Starr 1967).

John Hope Franklin is a man with a magnificent mind and a gentle manner.

ANALYTIC SUMMARY

The summary of this case study of the historian John Hope Franklin will focus on the various stages in his family, education, and career. The length of time required to complete each stage will be noted, as well as some of the significant events that linked the various stages in his life history.

The preschool and public school stages of Franklin's education were enhanced by the arrangement that involved his daily presence on the back bench of his mother's classroom. What he learned there gave Franklin a head start in his elementary and secondary education. He never lost this advantage, and he graduated at the top of his high school class.

Since he was precocious in developing reading and other cognitive skills, Franklin had time to develop some mechanical skills such as typing and shorthand, as well as self-confidence. This latter learning was beneficial in his education at the graduate level. Franklin finished the preschool and public school stages of his education in sixteen years.

The knowledge that Franklin's parents had of good centers of higher education available to blacks, along with the experience of his own brother, who attended Fisk University in Nashville, Tennessee, were significant in linking Franklin's public education to his college studies and in his wise choice of Fisk as his alma mater.

During the college stage Franklin was inspired intellectually, selected history as a vocation, learned to work as secretary to the librarian, and experienced a trusting relationship with a young woman whom he later married. His head start in reading and other cognitive skills was enhanced in college; and his self-confidence was deepened by the support he received from his history teacher, who became his mentor. Graduating magna cum laude, with a deepened sense of confidence, some knowledge of work, and evidence that teachers and companions are trustworthy, Franklin completed the college stage of higher education in four years.

The mentor's knowledge of Harvard University, his belief in Franklin's intellectual capacity, his advice to Franklin to apply to Harvard, and his securing of a bank loan to finance the first year of Franklin's graduate study were significant events and enabled Franklin to participate in the graduate school stage of the higher-education process. Franklin's good grades, his self-confidence, and his capacity to trust his mentor were other such events. Harvard's acceptance of Franklin was the final event that facilitated his further participation in graduate education.

Franklin emerged from graduate school with new knowledge: knowledge of different areas of the world; knowledge of various religious, social, and political movements and how they shape society; knowledge of how to transcend the effects of racism in an institution that is relatively insensitive to minorities; knowledge of how to work as a teacher; knowledge of how to do research; and knowledge of how to express oneself clearly in scientific papers that are publishable. Franklin assimilated this knowledge and these skills in six years.

Meanwhile, while he was doing research to complete his dissertation, Franklin had a job—an event that facilitated his transition from formal education to career development. The fact that the beginning of his career process overlapped the ending of his formal education contributed to the ease with which he could undertake marriage one year before receiving his doctoral degree.

Franklin's career also can be summarized in terms of stages of development. The beginning years of his career process were the eight years he spent at two different colleges in North Carolina, where he concentrated on teaching, research, and writing. The second stage of his career consisted of the nine years he spent at Howard University. There he refined his skills in teaching, research, and writing, and developed new skills in public affairs and in policy analysis. The third stage of his career consisted of his eight years at Brooklyn College. There he consolidated his earlier developed skills in teaching, research, writing, and public affairs; and developed new skills in administration. In the fourth stage of his career, at the University of Chicago, Franklin consolidated his earlier skills learned in North Carolina and Washington. He refined the administrative skills he had in New York and developed new skills in coordinating the growth and development of national learned societies. These sequences represent cycles in the pursuit of a professional career.

The career of John Hope Franklin as an ideal type demonstrates what a professional historian should do and when he or she should do it in order to achieve a career that can be described as "golden," "marvelous," and "a most satisfying intellectual experience."

As already mentioned, Franklin's career moved smoothly and with dispatch through the appropriate stages. It is possible that it progressed well because he initiated his career only two years before the final stage of his formal education ended. Further, he initiated marriage one year after his career had begun. These events occurred between the ages of twenty-four and twenty-six. The life of John Hope Franklin represents a creative interaction in time and space between the structured events of family, education, and career development.

CHAPTER 3

A Flexible and Many-Sided Economist

W. Arthur Lewis

HE IS A KNIGHT, decorated in 1963 at Buckingham Palace. His armament is his fine mind, which he uses well to benefit humanity. In recognition of this, Sir William Arthur Lewis was awarded the Nobel Prize in 1979 for his pioneering work in development economics. A reserved, quiet, mild-mannered man—honorable, strong-willed, tenaciously independent, and obstinate when necessary—he traveled with the high and mighty but had dedicated his career to understanding the economic situation of the meek and lowly.

A NEW ECONOMIC MODEL

In Lewis's words, "The vast majority of the world are poor. I was puzzled by this. I started from scratch and developed a new model for understanding this. In effect, the work I did in development repudiated my earlier work. My dissertation was in industrial economics."

Exploring and explaining development economics made sense in light of Lewis's background. W. Arthur Lewis was born in 1915 on St. Lucia, an island in the West Indies that at the time of his birth was part of the British colonial empire.

Economic models are useful and planning techniques are helpful. Lewis urges both the developing and the developed worlds to use these aids in "sensible policy-making" (Lewis 1966a, p.87). He counsels against "large and spectacular projects that cause considerable waste of capital" and, advocates "balanced growth [in public services and commodities], in the proportions dictated by demand [as] the right path," the sensible path to take by a developing country (Lewis 1966a pp.67–101).

A nation has its richer and poorer areas. This illustrates what John Rawls calls the principle of difference (Rawls 1971, p.101). A sensible economic plan invests the nation's resources in those areas with the best productive prospects, but also promotes full integration so that citizens who live in one area have a right to participate equally in economic activity in any part of their country. Even if there is full integration, Lewis explained, there will be resistance to the proposition that resources be invested where they are most productive. This resistance "derives from the expectation that those who live where the resources are invested are going to benefit most." Lewis, acknowledging that there is a reasonable basis for this expectation, suggests a way of minimizing it: "using some of the wealth produced in the richer areas to finance improved facilities in the poor areas, thus buying their consent to concentration of development policies in the area with the best prospects" (Lewis 1966a, p.69).

This idea shows Lewis's philosophical dimension. As a development economist, he is usually preoccupied with pragmatic concerns. Nevertheless, he is equally interested in philosophical inquiry because he believes that "economic growth depends both upon technological knowledge about things and living creatures, and also upon social knowledge about man and his relations with his fellow man" (Lewis 1955, p.164).

Lewis's recommendation for how to minimize resentment of a policy that concentrates national resources in those limited areas that offer the best prospects for productive development is confirmed by the philosophical analysis of others. John Rawls, philosopher and author of *A Theory of Justice*, observes that no individual merits greater natural capacity or deserves a more favorable starting place than any other. Yet these distinctions do not have to be eliminated to achieve fairness. According to Rawls, "the basic structure can be arranged so that these contingencies work for the good of the least fortunate." Since the superior potential for development of some areas is the result of circumstances for which no one can claim credit, no one should gain or lose because of his or her arbitrary place in the distribution of natural assets "without giving or receiving compensating advantages in return." In other words, "those who have been favored by nature . . . may gain from their good fortune only on terms that improve the situation of those who have lost out" (Rawls 1971, pp.101–104). Lewis's scheme provides for the giving and receiving of compensating advantages to obtain consent for an investment policy that is not universally applicable.

Development planning, as conceived by Lewis, is based on the "criterion of mutual benefit." From the standpoint of common sense, according to Rawls, this criterion should fulfill both the more advantaged and the less advantaged (Rawls 1971, p.104). This kind of planning must be fostered by the government. "No country," said Lewis, "has made economic progress without positive stimulus from intelligent governments" (Lewis 1955, p.366). Thus, "sensible people do not get involved in arguments about whether economic progress is due to government activity or to individual initiative; they know that it is due to both, and they concern themselves only with asking what is the proper contribution of each" (Lewis 1955, p.376). So goes the sensible economics of W. Arthur Lewis, who tells us that the "the secret of successful planning lies more in sensible politics and good public administration" (Lewis 1966a, p.7).

PEER AND PUBLIC RECOGNITION

Despite Lewis's mild manner and sensible approach, the brilliant formulation of his theory and his model of development economics has had a major influence in far-flung parts of the world. In our nationwide survey of minority and majority economists who are leaders in the field, Lewis was nominated as outstanding most frequently by scholars in both groups. When the names of four blacks who received multiple nominations was submitted to a random sample of ninety-eight members of predominantly white and predominantly black national economic organizations, an overwhelming vote of two-thirds identified W. Arthur Lewis as the most outstanding black scholar of economics in the United States. As mentioned before, his work in development economics was recognized when he received the Nobel Prize. Lewis has been recognized internationally by his professional peers and has been elected either president or vice-president of two nationwide professional associations in Ghana and the United States. Great Britain, which he served during the 1940s and early 1950s in a number of positions— including principal of the Board of Trade, member of the Colonial Economic Advisory Council, director of the Colonial Development Corporation, and member of the Departmental Commission on Fuel and Power—decorated him with the ancient and honorable title of Knight Bachelor.

An examination of the *Social Science Citation Index* for a two-year period, 1975 and 1976, attests to W. Arthur Lewis's extensive influence on the field of economics. Approximately twenty-one different works prepared by Lewis over the years were cited during this period by several authors in at least 106 social science journals. Lewis's study on labor in the West Indies, published in 1939, a year before he received his Ph.D. degree, was continuing to be cited a third of a century later. This fact testifies to the persisting value of the products of his scholarship.

Lewis's seminal article on "Economic Development with Unlimited Supplies of Labour," published in the *Manchester School* journal in May 1954, has also had a major impact. Among other themes, it analyzed the growth of profits and of savings relative to income. This article has been cited often over the years; during the two-year study period, it was cited in fifty-five different journals throughout the world, including *Journal of Economic Studies, American Economic Review, Oxford Bulletin of Economic Studies, and World Development,* among others. His book *The Theory of Economic Growth,* published in 1955, was cited eighteen times; and his 1966 book *Development Planning* was cited five times. Together, these three works accounted for two-thirds of the citations of works by W. Arthur Lewis listed in the 1976 *Social Science Citation Index.* There is nothing faddish about the scholarship of this economist. What he has written has endured. He is an economist for economists, most of whose work is cited by economists in economics journals.

FAMILY BACKGROUND

Home Community

The rise of a native son of the island of St. Lucia to such prominence as one of the world's leading economic scholars is an important story to tell. Indeed, his origins may hold part of the answer to the secret of the success of W. Arthur Lewis. His island home of 238 square miles was part of the British West Indies when he was a boy, and had a population of fewer than 100,000 people. The island was settled by the French in the late 1600s but came under the control of the British early in the 1800s. Although a British commissioner resided there until its colonial status was dissolved in 1979, French culture left an indelible mark. Arthur Lewis participated in these two cultures and in the indigenous folkways of the island people. He attended both British-oriented and French-oriented schools in his youth. These experiences undoubtedly contributed to his cosmopolitan outlook as well as to his concern for what happens to people in developing societies. In later years he researched and visited countries on several continents.

Family of Orientation

Probably a more profound influence on the education and career development of Lewis was his family of orientation. His mother was a major influence in his life. She managed to support the family with a dry goods business that she opened after Lewis's father died when Lewis was only seven. The household that George and Ida Lewis established included five sons, one of whom was W. Arthur Lewis.

"My parents were teachers," Lewis said. "They were educated in teacher-training schools in Antigua." Since the teacher-training course did not require four years of study, his mother and father attended college but did not graduate. Ida Lewis gave up teaching after she married but returned to the labor force as a business women when she was widowed: "I never found out how she managed to establish and support us; but she did, on the income from the business."

Lewis and his brothers had high aspriations and were encouraged to seek whatever education they needed to fulfill their vocational ambitions. "Going to England to study was not unusual for people in the British West Indies," Lewis said. When he went to England, he was not the first member of his family to go abroad for his education. One brother had gone away to study medicine; another went to Africa; still another studied law and became a judge.

Lewis's wife, Gladys Isabel Jacobs, who came from Grenada, also went to England to study. She and Lewis met there and made plans to marry. They had known of each other before since both families had roots in Antigua. Gladys Lewis's mother died when she was nine years old. Her father, a teacher who had attended a teacher-training college, wanted his four children to get a good education. He encouraged his daughter Gladys to go abroad. Her two brothers are professionals, a lawyer and a priest; her sister is married to a clergyman. Gladys finished a teacher-training program affiliated with the University of London, which also is the university home of the London School of Economics, where her husband-to-be first studied and later taught.

Family of Procreation

After completing her course of study in London, Gladys returned to Grenada. Lewis went there also for their wedding. The couple were married in 1947, when Lewis was thirty-two. Then they returned to London. Lewis was ten years beyond college, already had his Ph.D. degree, and had been a member of the faculty of the London School of Economics for six years. When the interview for this study was conducted, the Lewises had been married for thirty-four years.

Two daughters, to whom the Lewises are devoted, resulted from their union. The family often traveled together, with Mrs. Lewis and the children accompanying Professor Lewis because he did not want to leave the children behind with strangers. Of her husband, his work, and the family, Mrs. Lewis said, "He has always involved us somehow and we like it." She described her career as "being close to the family" so that her husband could work without unnecessary interruptions. However, she said, her husband would "come home and do things with the children such as taking the daughters for walks in the park." Both said that the presence of the children heightened any occasion, such as the time Sir Arthur was knighted, when the whole family went to Buckingham Palace for the ceremony.

The daughters have grown up, completed college, and pursued graduate education. One works in hospital administration, the other in computer science. As their mother stated, "They have moved out in the world." Their father mused, "I still enjoy them very much." The family of procreation that Gladys and Arthur Lewis established can be characterized as a warm and loving group of interdependent members who mutually sustain and support each other. Of his wife and children, Lewis said, "I cannot begin to speak of what I owe to their affection" (Lewis 1955, p.6).

EDUCATION

Lewis attended high school at St. Mary's College in St. Lucia, which he described as "a private Catholic school whose expenses were paid by the government." In 1933 he went to London to study for a bachelor's degree in commerce.

Lewis intended to be a lawyer. When he first enrolled in the London School of Economics, he said, "I had no idea what economics was." Many of his courses for the commerce degree had to do with law. In fact, he passed the first-level examination in law. Because of his good record as an undergraduate, Lewis was offered a scholarship by the London School of Economics to study for the Ph.D. degree in economics. The scholarship changed his vocational plans. Lewis doubted that he would have become an economist without it.

Thus at the age of twenty-two Lewis chose his vocation and committed himself to a rigorous course of graduate study in economics. Three years later he earned a doctoral degree without the preliminary step of earning a master's degree. Only twenty-five years old, Lewis had completed his formal education. His college and graduate school degrees were obtained from the same institution, the London School of Economics, which also recognized his talent sufficiently to offer him his first professional employment.

CAREER

Stage I

Just one year after be began studying for the doctoral degree, Lewis, then twenty-three, was appointed assistant lecturer at the London School of Economics. He worked at this rank for two years before his degree was officially awarded. Then he became lecturer and reader and remained as an official member of the faculty for a decade: "I stayed on to work in London because there was no employment then in the British Indies. I stayed on at the London School of Economics because the World War was on and there were not any offers from elsewhere. Also, I was going up the ladder with no difficulty."

Lewis climbed the career ladder with no difficulty not only because of the momentum he gained from his brilliant academic performance, but also because of his publications in the field of economics. In 1940, the year his Ph.D. degree was awarded, his first book was published, *Economic Problems of Today*. Reflecting on the first decade of his manhood, Lewis said, "There were not many blacks in Britain then." Now there are many blacks and Indians in British universities. Lewis, however, experienced no difficulty in obtaining employment: "After the initial appointment to the faculty of a British university, the burden is on the institution to prove that you should not be retained. Thus, reappointments are normal." After that, however, Lewis emphasized, one must establish oneself: "You cannot rely on the person who brought you to a place. You cannot be dependent on patronage. You have to establish yourself." This he did early on through his teaching, research, and writing: "My name got known in the profession because of articles I wrote in the early part of my career." At that time Lewis was still a bachelor and was able to concentrate fully on his studies and then on his developing career.

Stage II

The first five years of Lewis's professional career were devoted to teaching, research, and writing. Then, at twenty-eight, he moved into a second stage. Staying on at the London School of Economics

(Lewis commented that there is much less movement from university to university in the British system than in the U.S. system), he continued to refine his scholarly skills and added public policy-making to them. During the six-year period 1943–1949, while continuing to teach, he participated in the affairs of the government of the United Kingdom by serving as a principal of the Board of Trade, then Colonial Office, and as a director of the Colonial Advisory Council. Lewis's career was flourishing. He was recognized as a scholar in the university and as a man of public affairs in the United Kingdom.

By the time of his thirty-second birthday, Lewis's career was settling down well. That year, he married. The second stage in his career extended over a period of five years, from 1943 to 1948. He married one year before the end of this stage.

Stage III

In 1948, when he was thirty-three years old, another momentous event occurred: Lewis was offered an endowed chair as the Stanley Jevons Professor of Political Economy at the University of Manchester. Lewis explained that often in the British system one must go to a university other than the place one was initially appointed in order to get a full professorship. He remained at Manchester for a decade, including five years he spent on leave for assignments in Africa and elsewhere. He continued his teaching, research, and writing, and also expanded his participation in public affairs as a member of the Departmental Committee on Fuel and Power of the United Kingdom, as Economic Advisor to the Prime Minister of Ghana, and as president of the Economic Society of Ghana in 1958. During this stage, which lasted fifteen years, Lewis developed administrative skills by leaving the University of Manchester to serve as president of the University of the West Indies from 1959 to 1963. Meanwhile, his participation in public affairs was becoming world-wide in its significance. Near the end of this stage, Lewis served as deputy managing director of the United Nations Special Fund, while continuing on leave as president of the university.

In this period a change also occurred in Lewis's intellectual orientation. Although his dissertation was in applied economics, he shifted his focus during this period to development economics and constructed, as he described it, a new model "from scratch." In 1954 he published a significant article in the *Manchester School* journal on development; in 1955, when he was forty, he published a comprehensive treatise on *The Theory of Economic Growth*. The range of subject matter that had to be covered in this book was necessarily vast, but he felt compelled to tackle such an enormous task partly because of "irrepressible curiosity" and partly because of "the practical needs of contemporary policy-makers" (Lewis 1955, p.5). During this period Lewis discovered ways of linking his applied and theoretical interests in economics to enhance their effect on public policy.

These were activist years for Lewis, who described them as "taking large bits out of a life of scholarship." These remarks are especially relevant for the two years he spent in Africa on leave from his teaching position in Manchester, and the four years he spent as a university administrator in the West Indies. "When I came back to scholarship and research, I had to work doubly hard to get back into the field." Nevertheless, Lewis affirmed that what he was doing as an administrator was "worthwhile in its own terms. I learned much from administration: You learn that it is difficult to get people and institutions to change; there is no way to learn that except by being in the process. Administrative work teaches you how long it takes to get from A to B." Although he admitted that there is value in doing administrative jobs and that he learned much from administration, Lewis still contended that "administration and research are contradictory."

Stage IV

Thus in 1962, when the federation of Trinidad, Barbados, Jamaica, and other islands in the West Indies broke up, Lewis decided to return to research and teaching. Princeton University sent an emissary to the West Indies to deliver an invitation to Lewis to join its Department of Economics.

When he was forty-eight years old, Lewis accepted the Princeton invitation and moved to the United States to become James Madison Professor of Political Economy. While his contribution to the field continued with seven more books written or edited as a Princeton professor between 1963 and 1978 (making a total of twelve and an average of nearly one book every three years since the first was published in 1940), Lewis suddenly was showered with honors from everywhere. More universities in Africa, the United States, England, Europe, and the West Indies joined the growing list of those that had awarded him an honorary degree. He was decorated as a knight in 1963 and served as vice-president of the American Economic Association in 1965, at the age of fifty. Finally, his career was capped with the awarding of the Nobel Prize for his work in development economics in 1979, when he was sixty-four. Meanwhile, he managed to continue to use and develop his administrative skills. Between 1970 and 1973 he served on leave as president of the Caribbean Development Bank and then returned to Princeton.

Lewis looked forward to this stage in his career. By 1981 stage IV had spanned eighteen productive years. He considered the invitation from Princeton, in his words, "as an opportunity to stop sitting on committees and to get back to doing research." This he did without hesitation; during his first six years at Princeton he published four books—two in 1966 (*Politics of West Africa,* and *Development Planning*) and two in 1969 (*Some Aspects of Economic Development* and *Aspects of Tropical Trade, 1883–1965*).

Lewis's professional peers and the academy further recognized his scholarly achievements and conferred more honors on him during this stage. Lewis was elected distinguished fellow in the American Economic Association and its president in the early 1980s. Manchester University, where he was first appointed as full professor, awarded him an honorary Doctor of Science degree in 1973, twenty-five years after he first came to it. This degree, together with the one he received from the University of the West Indies in 1966, means that two of the four institutions of higher education in which Sir Arthur Lewis worked have given him one of their highest honors. And in 1984, he capped this stage in his career with an honorary doctorate from Harvard Univesity.

PERSONAL CHARACTERISTICS

What manner of man is W. Arthur Lewis? Earlier he was character-ized as a quiet, mild-mannered person. The record also shows that he is a sensible and serious scholar and a determined man who has worked hard to merit the opportunities that have come his way. His determination could take on the character of a driving obsession were it not tempered by a genuine capacity for gratitude. He is quick to express his indebtedness to others, including his family and his professional colleagues (both those he knows and those unknown to him personally), and his gratitude for their assistance that facilitated his work.

His achievements far exceed the requirements of the situations in which he found himself. In this respect he can be classified as an overachiever. There is purpose to his hard work and extraordinary effort. Lewis recalled that when he went to England, not many blacks were in British universities. Years later, when he came to the United States, he discovered that Princeton had a reputation for discri-mination. He thought that it would be of value to overcome these barriers. Lewis believed that he personally had to establish himself in order to overcome—that he could not depend on patronage or any other support system.

Lewis set out to establish himself by going beyond the call of duty in all his undertakings. Consequently, he ascended the ladder without impediments wherever he was, in both English and U.S. universities. He felt compelled to do this because he always wanted to be in a position "to quit tomorrow and still get a job." The realization that he could do this because of the quality of his work has made a big difference in his career, Lewis said. His belief in this goal is the basis for describing him as tenaciously independent.

Lewis also should be described as a flexible person who is capable of changing when the circumstances and conditions of his life warrant it. He described his movement into development economics in the 1950s as a repudiation of much of his earlier work. He did not consider this unusual and conjectured that "it must happen to a lot of scholars." Unfortunately, many scholars are not so flexible. Some resist accepting new interpretations even when the facts demonstrate that old interpretations are wrong. Lewis, demonstrably is not one of these.

In his theoretical book in 1955, Lewis asserted that no country had made economic progress without positive stimulus from intelligent governments. However, after observing "the cruel events of the year 1966" in Nigeria, and before the outcome of the civil war in that nation became clear, he asserted that "economic progress depends more on people and resources than it does on governments." This assertion, slightly at variance with the earlier one, was based on experience. During the years after writing *The Theory of Economic Growth*, Lewis observed in many places that a common currency, unrestricted transportation, and a minimum of bureaucratic licensing are essentials for economic growth (Lewis 1967, p.5). His analysis was that Nigeria was likely to retain these despite breakdown in its government. If it could do so, he said, economic development should resume after the war, since "this resulted more from the adaptability of the farmers, the energy of the business community, and the resources of the country, than from anything that the governments were doing" (Lewis 1967, p.5).

Lewis assigns a high place to experience and pragmatics as well as to theory and philosophy in his economic analysis. Consequently, he tries to provide both operational guidelines and theoretical concepts. Economics has turned out to be a mathematical science. At one point in his career he served as president of the Manchester Statistical Society. Yet he feels comfortable writing a book "for the intelligent layman." "Very little has appeared on how a development plan is made, what the chief snags are, and what distinguishes good planning from bad," he said. The person in the street whose life is affected by those plans needs "a short and simple introduction" that can help him. Lewis gave himself the task of doing this in his book on *Development Planning* (1966a), just as he had assigned himself the task of preparing *The Theory of Economic Growth* (1955) because it was needed by policymakers.

Lewis, a pragmatist and a philosopher, has pitched his career in the direction in which it has moved not so much for fame and fortune as for the purpose of being helpful and serving others by filling a void with needed information. To follow a career pattern like the one

Lewis has followed is possible only among those who are self-confident. Apparently Lewis's socialization and early experiences nurtured the development of such confidence, which in turn has contributed to his sense of freedom and flexibility in determining what to study and how to present his results.

ANALYTIC SUMMARY

This summary will focus largely on the family, education, and career development of W. Arthur Lewis and the interaction between these three systems.

The birth of a black person into a household that lived in a British possession during the age of colonialism was a significant event in that it established the conditions that one had to overcome. Within his kinship system the educational accomplishments of Lewis's mother and father during an age when few blacks received postsecondary education indicate their orientation toward achievement, which obviously was passed on to their offspring.

The death of his father when Lewis was only seven years old must have created a serious void in his family, but the extraordinary compensating behavior of his mother succored and sustained him and his siblings. She had to go into the labor force as a self-employed businesswoman to do this. Consequently, she was able to provide an umbrella of safety and security for the members of her family until they left the household after college. One may call stage I in the kinship system the period of nurturance in the family of orientation. For Lewis this period extended through the completion of college, the end of stage III in the education system.

For the next ten years Lewis withdrew from the direct care of his family of orientation and moved into what became for him a transitional independent-household stage II. During this stage Lewis initiated and completed stage IV in the education system, his graduate education. Lewis completed this stage and received his Ph.D. degree in the record time of only three years. The stage of graduate study in the higher-education process began immediately after Lewis had completed the college stage III at the age of twenty-two.

Two years before he received the Ph.D. degree, Lewis received his first professional appointment, as assistant lecturer, which launched his professional career into stage I of that system at the age of twenty-three. He moved rapidly in five years through stage I in career development—teaching, doing research, and writing. When Lewis was twenty-eight, he began stage II of his career, which lasted another five years. Although he remained at the London School of Economics, Lewis became a full lecturer and reader; refined the skills he had developed in teaching, research, and writing; and branched out into public affairs as a policymaker. All this occurred while Lewis was in stage II of the kinship system, occupying the position of an independent householder. He was able to concentrate on education and career development because of the absence of family responsibility in the kinship system.

One year before he moved into stage III of his career, which took on worldwide significance for a period of more than fifteen years, Lewis married. Thus stage III, the family of procreation, was launched by Lewis one year before he began stage III of his professional career. Lewis was thirty-two years old when he married and thirty-three when he received his first appointment as full professor at Manchester University.

Stage III in Lewis's career development consolidated his earlier skills in teaching, research, and writing; refined the policymaking skills that he had begun developing in stage II; and initiated the development of new skills in administration. Moreover, Lewis assumed leadership responsibility for the growth and development of his discipline as a national leader of a professional association. His book-publishing activity continued during this stage, bringing the number of books written to five.

Lewis did all this so well that he was decorated as a knight as stage IV of his career began. Stage IV brought Lewis to the United States, where he has served with distinction as the James Madison Professor of Political Economy at Princeton University until his retirement in the early 1980s. At the time of this study, stage IV had lasted eighteen years. The other public honor of note that was to come his way during stage IV was the Nobel Prize for his pioneering work in development economics, and his election as president of the American Economic Association.

During stage IV, which began when he was forty-eight years old, Lewis continued to develop as a scholar. In addition to teaching, he did research and authored or edited seven more books, bringing the total to twelve. He was elected vice-president and president of the American Economic Association, and attained the status of distinguished fellow of that association. He served for three years (on leave from Princeton) as president of the Caribbean Development Bank; and he accepted membership on the Economic Advisory Council of the National Association for the Advancement of Colored People (NAACP) in the United States. Finally, he was the recipient of many public honors, including an honorary doctoral degree from Harvard in 1984. Thus one could call stage IV in Lewis's career development a stage of consolidation.

All during stages III and IV in his career, stage III in his kinship system—the family of procreation—remained intact. This fact undoubtedly had a stabilizing effect on him. The affection he received from his wife and two daughters obviously sustained him through the many moves and responsibilities required in the development of a career devoted to the service of others in scholarship, public affairs, administration, and leadership of learned societies.

CHAPTER 4

A Psychologist Committed to Justice and Equality

Kenneth B. Clark

FOR MORE THAN FIFTEEN YEARS a member of the powerful Board of Regents that oversees education in New York State, Kenneth Bancroft Clark is a scholar who has had a profound effect on public policy and public education in this nation. Since the midpoint of the twentieth century and the landmark U.S. Supreme Court decision in *Brown* v. *Board of Education*, Clark's reputation has soared. That decision, delivered by Chief Justice Earl Warren on May 17, 1954, outlawed segregated public education in the United States and was influenced in part by the research findings of Clark.

The *Brown* decision reversed the Court's interpretation of the law fifty-eight years earlier. The Fourteenth Amendment to the Constitution guarantees equal protection of the law to all citizens. In 1896, however, in *Plessy* v. *Ferguson*, the U.S. Supreme Court ruled that this clause of the Constitution could be fulfilled under conditions of state-sanctioned segregation, if facilities and services for the various racial populations were equal though separate.

BROWN V. BOARD OF EDUCATION

The 1954 decision declared that education is perhaps the most important function of state and local governments and that it is

41

doubtful that any child may reasonably be expected to succeed in life if he or she is denied the opportunity for an education. The Court then examined the effect of segregation itself on public education. After analyzing the evidence, the Court stated its belief that segregation of children in public schools solely on the basis of race, even though the physical facilities and other tangible factors may be equal, deprives the children of the minority group of equal educational opportunity. Further, the Court indicated that to separate black children in grade and high school from others of similar age and qualification, solely because of their race, generates a feeling of inferiority with respect to their status in the community that may affect their hearts and minds in a way unlikely ever to be undone. The Court said that this finding is amply supported by modern authority (*Brown* v. *Board of Education*, 1954).

In a footnote to the decision, Kenneth B. Clark headed the list of modern social science authorities whose findings were cited and used by the Court in arriving at its unanimous opinion that "separate educational facilities are inherently unequal." The reference was listed this way: K. B. Clark, Effect of Prejudice and Discrimination on Personality Development (Mid-Century White House Conference on Children and Youth, 1950).

The Mid-Century White House Conference on Children and Youth actually met in 1951. Clark summarized the material he had reviewed in the White House Conference report for the appendix of the appellants' brief in the *Brown* case. The appellants' brief was prepared by the legal staff of the National Association for the Advancement of Colored People (NAACP). That appendix, entitled "The Effects of Segregation and the Consequences of Desegregation: A Social Science Statement," was endorsed by thirty-two social scientists, psychologists, and psychiatrists (Clark 1974, p.93). In addition, as a social science consultant to the NAACP, Clark examined black children involved in several of the cases that were combined in the *Brown* decision "to determine whether evidence of personality distortion related to racial discrimination and segregation could be ascertained" (Clark 1974, p. 93). His own assessment of the impact of social science evidence is reported: "The introduction of social science testimony in these cases," he said, "proved to be significant extension of legal frontiers" (Clark 1974, p.93). Others, however, such as social psychologist Richard Evans, said that Clark's "contributions to the literature on prejudice and the effects of segregation on blacks in America . . . influenced . . . our entire culture through [their] impact on the Supreme Court's decision" (Evans 1980, p.63).

TEACHING AND COMMUNITY SERVICE

Clark has been an activist psychologist in search of justice and equality, moral and ethical truths. From the earliest days of his career, he has pursued these goals, never compromising them even at the risk of losing a job. Immediately after receiving his doctoral degree, Clark went South to teach in a predominantly black college whose president suggested that his "brand of psychology" was contributing to the frustration of students in that he was not helping them "adjust to the realities of American racism." Clark told the president that he could not do this, and left the position. Thus Clark lasted less than a year in what could have been his first permanent professional appointment.

City College of New York (later known as City College of the City University of New York) accepted Clark on his own terms as an activist social scientist interested both in teaching and community service. Clark remained at City College throughout his entire professional career as a teacher. From time to time he served as visiting professor at other schools, such as Columbia, Harvard, and the University of California at Berkeley; but he always returned to City College, which understood and supported him.

Clark has been recognized nationwide by professional organizations and has served as president of two of the leading learned associations of psychology in the United States. His influence has been nationwide and particularly significant over a long period of time on public-policy issues in New York State and in New York City.

Clark believes that the social sciences and social psychology should be and must be "instruments by which people seek to help their fellow human beings" (Evans 1980, p.71). In Clark's community service (such as the work he and his wife did at the Northside Center for Child Development, co-founded by them; Harlem Youth Opportunities Unlimited, which he served as chairman and project director; and the Metropolitan Applied Research Center, which he organized), he has acted out this belief. He has identified the prime goal of social science as "helping society move toward humanity and justice, with minimum irrationality, instability, and cruelty" (Clark 1965 pp.xxi–xxii).

Clark obtained great satisfaction from teaching, but he also pursued research to achieve the goals mentioned earlier. His community-service and public-affairs activities have left less time than he would prefer to write up his observations and to share them with other colleagues. Nevertheless, he has written and edited about seven books and many articles, including a prize-winning book, *Dark Ghetto*, that earned him the Sidney Hillman Book Award in 1965.

Clark does not apologize for his applied work because he believes that social scientists must "demonstrate the validity of hope" (Clark 1974, p.xii). This he believes, is essential "to the survival of the human species" (Clark 1974, p.xii). Because he sees his professional work as having to do with the business of survival, he does not see his involvement in public-policy issues as separate from his work as a social psychologist: "There is not a clear distinction between social psychology and social action; they are one and the same."

Yet Clark is aware that some professional psychologists take a contrary view. The controversy engendered by his participation in the adversarial school-desegregation court cases was sufficient evidence of the negative view that some of the most respected psychologists in the field have of social action and applied social psychology. With full knowledge of the possible professional costs, Clark has continued his dual activity of social science research and social action. Consequently, Clark was genuinely surprised when he was nominated to be president of the American Psychological Association. He had thought that many would dismiss his social action as being of little social science value.

Our study confirms that Kenneth Clark's brand of psychology has been accepted as worthy by many. When both black and white leaders in psychology were asked to nominate three outstanding black psychologists for our study, Clark's name was mentioned the most frequently. When the names of the three psychologists who received the most nominations were submitted to a random sample of eighty-seven members of black and of white national professional organizations in psychology, 80 percent of the study population ranked Clark as the most outstanding black psychologist. Thus there is consensus in the discipline that Clark indeed has made major contributions to psychology.

One can say that Clark has pioneered in helping to transform social psychology into a field that takes seriously moral and ethical dilemmas in human behavior, and that applies its findings for ameliorative effect. Moreover, he has succeeded in effectively transcending barriers of resistance to these concerns. His selection in 1978 at the age of sixty-four as the first recipient of the Award for Distinguished Contribution to Psychology in the Public Interest is evidence supporting the assertion that Clark has persevered and has prevailed.

FAMILY BACKGROUND

How did one who grew up imprisoned in a New York city black ghetto, where material rewards are hard to come by and where the motives of almost everyone are suspect, eventually become a significant source of information for the U.S. Supreme Court and a national president of the American Psychological Association? How did one who attended the Harlem public schools, in which a guidance counselor in junior high school tried unsuccessfully to steer him into a vocational high school, earn membership in Phi Beta Kappa and Sigma Xi, and receive election by the state legislature to the Board of Regents? How did one whose family moved from house to house and from neighborhood to neighborhood in a desperate attempt to escape the ghetto's creeping blight become so stable and steady in adulthood, remaining at one place of employment, City University of New York, for thirty-three years and eventually retiring as Distinguished University Professor Emeritus? The simple answer, according to Kenneth Clark, is two women in his life—his mother and his wife.

Family of Orientation

Miriam Hanson Clark brought her two children to New York City from the Panama Canal Zone, where they were born, when Kenneth Clark was four years old and his sister a year old. Clark's parents were born in Jamaica, but their separate families had migrated to the Canal Zone in search of work. His mother and father met and married there, where his father worked as a superintendent of cargo with the United Fruit Company.

Eventually Arthur and Miriam Clark separated. Clark's mother, whom he described as "very firm, forthright, and ambitious," wanted her children to have good educational opportunities. She felt that these could not be obtained in the Canal Zone. Without family connections to keep her there, she decided to seek out new opportunities for her young household in New York City, where she had a sister (Clark 1978, p.79).

In 1918 Miriam Clark moved to New York with her infant daughter and young son. She found work in the garment district as a dressmaker by day, took care of her family, and went to school at night. Eventually she received a diploma from the evening division of George Washington High School—the same school from which her son would graduate at the age of sixteen as a student in the daytime program.

George Washington High School has much meaning in the current Clark household. Kenneth and Mamie Clark set up a scholarship at the school in memory of Clark's mother, whom Clark called "a strong woman." He recalled an incident before he enrolled in high school that indicates his mother's strong orientation toward education. After learning that the junior high school counselor was trying to steer her son into a vocational rather than an academic high school (the counselor's way of advising black youngsters to be "realistic" about their employment options), Clark's mother stormed into school one day and said to the counselor: "I don't care where you send your son, but mine is going to George Washington High School." Clark said that his mother was not awed by authority and that her daring ways saved him and his sister (Clark 1978 pp.79–80).

Clark's mother told him and his sister that they had to go to college. To prepare for college, she insisted, they must get good grades in school; she believed that Clark would either get good grades or end up in jail. Clark reflected with amusement, "She didn't give me any middle ground."

She did let Clark decide which college he would attend. Clark chose Howard University in Washington, D.C., where he had some scholarship money and thus did not have to work his way through college. His mother gave him her full support. She worked to put him and his sister through college, and also provided some support for graduate school.

Clark's mother wanted him to study for the priesthood in the Episcopal Church. But when he told her that he had decided to major in psychology, although she did not know what psychology was, she did not express disappointment; she merely said, "Whatever you do, do it well." Clark understood what she meant.

Family of Procreation

Clark met Mamie Phipps at Howard, where she was a freshman when he was a senior. When she told him then that he was going to be a great psychologist, Clark dismissed her remarks as "courtship talk." Over the years, however, she has acted in accordance with this assessment; in Clark's words, "she has done everything she could to make her prophecy come true." Clark has found her efforts in his behalf a great support.

Kenneth and Mamie Clark married in 1938. He was twenty-four, had earned his M.S. degree in psychology from Howard, and was just two years shy of his Ph.D. degree at Columbia. She had just graduated from college, and she continued her education; after finishing her master's degree at Howard, she came to New York and eventually became the first black women to receive a Ph.D. in psychology from Columbia University.

The Clarks' two children have grown into adulthood and have offspring of their own. The Clarks have a summer home on Cape Cod where the clan frequently gathers, away from the pressures of the New York City metropolitan area. At the time of this interview, in 1981, the family of procreation created by Kenneth and Mamie Clark had continued as a steady, stable, and supportive unit for forty-three years. Kenneth Clark attributes the many years of their effective union in marriage to the fact that his wife is so honest: "She will tell you exactly how she feels." As they have done over the years, the Clarks continue to work together both personally and professionally.

Mamie Phipps Clark died in 1983. She was survived by her husband and their two offspring—Kate Harris and Hilton Clark. A letter of condolence to Kenneth Clark and his family mentioned Mamie as "a model of a concerned, compassionate and caring person" who had a great love affair with her family.

Miriam Clark, the mother, and Mamie Clark, the wife, are the two people Kenneth Clark has characterized as "strong women who demanded of me the maximum." There was no break in the nurturance that Clark received from strong women. One took over where the other left off.

EDUCATION

Preschool, Primary School, and Secondary School

Clark's preschool and primary education occurred on streets and playgrounds and in Harlem schools. Clark described his early years this way: "I started school in the Harlem public schools. I first learned about people, about love, and cruelty, about sacrifice, about cowardice, about courage, about bombast in Harlem" (Clark 1965, p.xv). On the basis of this testimony, one must conclude that Harlem provided a comprehensive education and a range of advice. In fact, Clark's choice of Howard University for his college studies was based on information he received from a Harlem playground attendant who was a medical school student at Howard.

Clark does not remember much about his primary and secondary school teachers. One who stood out, however, was Mr. Dixon, a junior high school speech teacher and the first person who let Clark know that he could take ideas and transform them into words in which other people would be interested. After a three-minute speech that Dixon had assigned, Clark remembers, his teacher was "very positive in his reaction to it." Dixon asked Clark to enter an essay contest sponsored by a baking company. Although he cannot recall what he wrote, Clark remembers that for his essay he won a gold medal that was presented to him during assembly period: "I was very proud and Mr. Dixon was proud too." In summary, Clark said of his primary and secondary schooling, "I remember the names of only the teachers I admired" (Clark 1978, p.79).

Clark also admired his playground attendant. He described her as "a medical student at Howard University in Washington, D.C." (Clark 1978, p.80). She depicted Howard to him as a school where blacks were in control. Before his college years, Clark had never

found himself in a setting where blacks were in control of anything—
not even Harlem. "Blacks certainly were not in control in New York
when I was growing up," Clark said. For example, there were only
ten black students in his high school senior class in New York.

B.A. and M.A.

Clark enrolled at Howard University during the Depression and
graduated in 1935, when he was almost twenty-one. He found
Howard exciting, personally, socially, and intellectually. He enu-
merated the intellectual giants there with whom he came into
contact: Kelly Miller in education, Ralph Bunche in political science,
Charles Houston in law, Alain Lock in philosophy, Abram Harris in
economics, Sterling Brown in English, and Francis Cecil Sumner in
psychology: "These teachers made their students into instruments of
change." The teachers were able to accomplish this goal, he said,
because they were "our tutors, models, and friends. They were
affecting our lives, goals, values. They remained my friends until
death."

Clark reserved special praise for Francis Cecil Sumner. "For
me," said Clark, "Sumner was the key at Howard." Clark had
enrolled at Howard intending to become a physician, but during his
sophomore year he enrolled in Sumner's course in Introductory
Psychology. Clark started listening to the ideas of this psychology
professor, who had studied for the doctorate at Clark University in
Worcester, Massachusetts.

Sumner was strong on content and substance: "He was the best
read person I ever knew. His discussions about man and society
caught my attention. Sumner got me interested about man and the
world." Though soft-spoken, "Sumner was uncompromising in
insistence on high standards of the students worthy of his attention. I
respected the man. I admired him. I leaned on him. He became my
mentor and my friend. I became his protégé. Sumner continued to be
interested in all that happened to me. He was happy when Mamie
and I got married." Sumner had a newsletter that he sent around
about his former students, detailing their progress.

Clark attributes his life-long vocation in psychology to Sumner's
influence: "My sophomore year, after listening to Sumner, I
immediately decided that I would not continue in my premedical
studies. I started taking more courses in psychology and physiology. I
never turned back, although I did not go to Howard to major in
psychology." After receiving his bachelor's degree, Clark remained at
Howard for a year of study for the M.S. degree in psychology. He
then taught at Howard as Sumner's protégé. It was Sumner who
advised Clark to go away to get his Ph.D. after he had taught at
Howard for a year.

Ph.D. Study

Clark moved on to Columbia University to study for the doctoral degree in psychology. He entered Columbia in 1937 and graduated three years later, at the age of twenty-six.

One reason Clark chose Columbia was his encounter with Otto Klineberg in Washington when Klineberg was a guest lecturer at Howard. Clark was impressed with Klineberg's candor and directness. He was pleased to observe these characteristics in a white person; few talked the way Klineberg did in his lecture on racial differences: "I suppose I wanted to go into the field that Otto Klineberg was in." Clark studied with Klineberg, who became his mentor and friend, and also with Gardner Murphy.

Clark was able to move through Columbia rapidly because he found "no challenges at Columbia that were more challenging than the standards of Sumner." According to Clark, however, some professors at Columbia were "surprised and amazed that a black could meet their standards and even surpass them." At Columbia he was invited to join Sigma Xi, and he ranked first among those who took the qualifying examination with him for the Ph.D. degree. The head of the program was "so amazed" that he summoned Clark to his office and interrogated him; he asked Clark to account for the fact that he had come out ahead of all the others who took the examination. None of these attitudes and actions hampered Clark's progress. "It was preordained that I would do well at Columbia when I studied for my Ph.D. degree, because of Sumner."

Although he is best known for his contributions to the literature on prejudice and the effects of segregation on blacks in the United States, Clark did not do research on race for his dissertation. He studied selective perception, selective recall, and attitudes, and how these influence human behavior. His dissertation was entitled "Some Factors Influencing the Remembering of Prose Material" (Clark 1940). The research, despite its bland title, was not totally unrelated to what would later become Clark's major research interest. In his dissertation research, Clark determined the extent to which attitudes toward females who violated stereotypical pictures of the female affected groups of subjects' recall. He found that both men and women tended to remember these females more in terms of the feminine stereotypes than in terms of the original stimulus (Evans 1980, p.65). Evident in Clark's dissertation research is an underlying concern with stereotyping and other issues that he would later consider in his studies of race.

Clark's interest in injustice had been awakened at Howard. The faculty there was extraordinary, but Clark soon learned that these outstanding scholars had congregated at Howard because they could not get appointments to the faculties of Harvard University or Clark

University or wherever they had received their Ph.D. degrees. "I learned from the discussions at Howard that these men could not teach anyplace other than a predominantly black school." This realization, he said, was "a turning point for me." Clark did not pursue his awakened interest in injustice immediately, however, because his professors at Columbia suggested that it would be desirable for him "not to come on too strong" in his concern with racial justice.

Some teachers at predominantly white universities may discourage blacks from emphasizing issues of race while they are in residence, but at graduation time race is these teachers prevailing thought with respect to placement. For example, Clark said, "when I had finished my graduate studies at Columbia, I was asked if I was going back to teach my people. I told my Columbia professors," Clark recalled, "that my people were all around and I wanted to be recommended for wherever they recommended Columbia graduates." One person who graduated with him already had been recommended for a prestigious private university in the East. That person obviously had not performed as well as Clark; and, Clark said, "I let the people at Columbia know that."

CAREER

"The people at Columbia settled on City College as the school to which I would be recommended," Clark said. Gardner Murphy, one of Clark's teachers at Columbia, was to become the chairman of the Department of Psychology at City College. Although Murphy welcomed his former student to the City College faculty, he still looked on the appointment of a black professor " as experimental," Clark said. Clark himself experimented with one or two other employment settings after graduating from Columbia, including teaching for less than a year at Hampton Institute, working with Gunnar Myrdal, and working with the Office of War Information. Unhappy with the circumstances and conditions of employment elsewhere, he sought out the City College option in 1942. It was still available, and he accepted an appointment initially to the rank of instructor. Clark was twenty-eight, had received his Ph.D. degree two years earlier, and at that time was in the fourth year of his marriage. Thus City University became the first full-time permanent job in his unfolding career.

Stage I

The first stage in Clark's career lasted from 1942 to 1950. During this eight-year period he immersed himself in teaching, research, and community service. Mamie Clark observed that her husband really thrives on teaching. Kenneth Clark agreed that teaching was so uplifting that he could go into a classroom with a headache or a cold, "and within ten or fifteen minutes I was feeling wonderful." The students he remembers are those who brought to their studies "a passionate sensitivity and critical probing intelligence." Clark said that Francis Cecil Sumner, his first psychology teacher at Howard, was the model he emulated (Clark 1978, p.83).

Teaching has been so important in his life and career that Clark classified as his "most important contribution" his students—what they have done as a result of what he has done. Specifically, Clark indicated satisfaction with his students who "take seriously the responsibility of using social science as an instrument for helping their fellow human being" (Evans 1980, p.71).

This is precisely what he and his psychologist wife Mamie Clark tried to do in their first community-service venture—the Northside Child Development Center, which they cofounded in 1946. She directed the center, and Clark signed on as research director while continuing to teach full time at City College. They were literally trying to save underprivileged children in Harlem by "building the sense of self as an integral part of . . . psychotherapy" (Evans 1980, p.68).

The Clarks' research agenda at that time was one on which Mamie Clark had been working while pursuing the master's degree. Her thesis research was a study of self-awareness. Extending this research and developing new instruments, Kenneth and Mamie Clark used dolls and the color test to explore ways that black children develop a sense of their own identity. This research, begun in the initial stage of Clark's career, was written up and first published by him and his wife in 1947 under the title "Racial Identification and Preference in Negro Children" (Clark and Clark 1947). Clark was thirty-three when that article was published. Although his research was progressing well, he did not publish extensively during the first eight years of his career. Teaching, research, and community service were his preoccupations.

Stage II

By Clark's own reckoning, the most active part of his career commenced around 1950 (Clark 1978, p.83). This began stage II, which lasted a decade, roughly from 1950 through 1959 and Clark's forty-fifth birthday. Beginning when he was thirty-six this stage started with his research for the Mid-Century White House Conference on Children and Youth. The report that Clark prepared for the White House Conference, in turn, led to his appointment as a social science consultant to the NAACP. In addition to continuing his teaching, research, and community service, Clark increased his writing activity and became deeply involved in public-policy matters through his work with the NAACP on its school-desegregation court cases.

Clark describes the sequence of events that launched stage II of his career. His Columbia University advisor, Otto Klineberg, was a member of the Advisory Committee of the Mid-Century White House Conference on Children and Youth. On Klineberg's recommendation, Clark -was asked about two or three months before the conference to synthesize the literature on the effects of race, prejudice, discrimination, and segregation on personality development of children in the United States. Meanwhile, lawyers for the NAACP turned to Klineberg for help in establishing as a fact the inherent psychological damage segregation caused for blacks, even when facilities for the different racial populations might be equal. Klineberg referred Robert Carter, who was Thurgood Marshall's assistant, to Clark because of the work Clark had done for the White House Conference. Carter was excited about the material in Clark's report and its relevance to the school-desegregation cases (Evans 1980, p.66–67).

The NAACP then signed Clark on as a consultant, and Clark began advising the lawyers concerning social scientists who would be good expert witnesses. He interviewed children and prepared the social science appendix for the lawyers' brief. He summarized the essential points of the testimony of the expert witnesses during the trial. Also included in the appendix was material contained in Clark's report for the White House Conference on Children and Youth. The social science appendix was submitted to the Supreme Court as part of the brief prepared by the NAACP in the *Brown* case. Clark described his involvement in that historical case as "a highlight" of his career (Clark 1978, p.84). This was part of his effort to integrate research activities with applied services, which he feels is another of his contributions to psychology.

Clark praised the City College Department of Psychology for being extraordinarily supportive of his public-policy work with the NAACP in connection with the *Brown* case: "My colleagues competed to substitute for me in my courses so that I could be away and work on the case. They thought it was an honor for one of their faculty to be involved in a case as important as this." Some of the administrators, however, were not as pleased. One called him in for a conference on the matter. After the conversation, Clark told the administrator, "If you are asking me to make a choice between continuing to work with the lawyers of NAACP or with City College, I am certain what choice I will make." The City College administrator retreated.

Following the U.S. Supreme Court's decision in 1954, Clark published his first important book, *Prejudice and Your Child* (1955), a revision of the report he had prepared for the Mid-Century White

House Conference on Children and Youth, on which the Supreme Court had in part based its school-desegregation opinion. Clark was forty-one years old, and his career was accelerating. During this stage he refined his teaching and research skills, further cultivated his writing skills, and learned how to participate effectively in public-policy matters.

Stage III

When he turned forty-five, Clark's career was moving full speed ahead into stage III, which was characterized by teaching, research, writing, public-affairs activities, community service, administration, and leadership of a national learned association. It also was the stage in which he would begin receiving some of the many public honors that would come his way.

As the opening event in this stage of his career, Clark served as president of the Society for the Psychological Study of Social Issues in 1959. The turbulent 1960s were about to begin. As a reward for his past contributions to the academic community, Clark was promoted to the rank of full professor at City College of the City University of New York in 1960, at the age of forty-six. Stage III of Clark's career covered the decade of the 1960s.

During the 1960s Clark did many things and did them well. He chaired and served as project director of the massive delinquency-prevention planning project in Harlem that was sponsored by the President's Committee on Juvenile Delinquency and Youth Crime and by the mayor of New York City. In the service that he and Mamie Clark had rendered earlier at the Northside Center for Child Development, it became clear to them that something would have to be done about the environment. Harlem Youth Opportunities Unlimited (HARYOU) was one structure through which Clark attempted to accomplish this end. This service-planning project in Harlem, where Clark had spent more than forty years, was the final demonstration for him that a social scientist "could never be fully detached" (Clark 1965, p.xv).

In the course of the delinquency-prevention planning project, Clark also learned that political forces could move in and sap a project's vitality. This was a dimension of power of which he had been largely unaware (Evans 1980, p.68). In an earlier stage of his career, he had seen political force, by way of the Supreme Court, make available in an equitable way a public service, education. Now, in the third stage of his career, he was witnessing political considerations that were impeding the full implementation of massive public services for a community.

Kenneth Clark has the capacity to turn his liabilities into assets. As he withdrew from the HARYOU project after the planning phase so that it could be merged with another community-service project in Harlem, Associated Community Teams (ACT), for the implementation phase, he reflected on all that he had learned in Harlem and in other ghetto communities and wrote a prize-winning book, *Dark Ghetto* (1965), that presented a profound and insightful analysis of ghetto life and its meaning to ghetto dwellers. The book received the Sidney Hillman Book Award for 1965.

That same year, 1965, Clark received the Kurt Lewin Memorial Award by the Society for the Psychological Study of Social Issues. His acceptance address, entitled "Problems of Power and Social Change: Toward a Relevant Social Psychology," was an analysis of the role of power in social organization and a challenge to his colleagues in social psychology to cease investigating isolated, trivial, and convenient problems and to start studying problems directly related to urgent social realities (Clark 1974, p.68). In this speech Clark conveyed the wisdom he had obtained from both his successes and his failures in dealing with political power. He urged his professional contemporaries to "accept power as an important concept for research" (Clark 1974, p.69).

During this stage of his career, in 1966, Clark was elected by the legislature to the powerful Board of Regents of New York State. He would serve on that board for nearly two decades, giving oversight to all aspects of education in the state. Meanwhile, Clark's talents were recognized beyond his state. The federal government asked him to serve on the Committee on Foreign Affairs Personnel of the State Department, and the NAACP gave him the Spingarn Medal, one of its most prestigious awards.

Also during this time, Clark established an organization that would draw on and consequently develop his administrative skills. In 1967 he became president of the Metropolitan Applied Research Center (MARC), a private nonprofit research corporation established to serve as a catalyst for change and as an advocate for the poor and powerless in U.S. cities. MARC was called an experiment. Possibly its grandest plan was the design of an Academic Achievement Project for public schools in the District of Columbia. The plan was based on the assumption that all normal children can learn if they are taught effectively. The plan specified radical ways in which the local school system would have to be restructured, reorganized, and staffed to accomplish the stated goal. It was never implemented. However, the plan has been published by Clark and the staff of MARC so that others may review it and use those aspects that can be accommodated in their local communities (Clark 1972). MARC was one more illustration that Kenneth Clark refused to limit his activities to the ivory tower. In addition to his contributions as a scholar, Clark always has needed a community-service outlet. When available associations were not appropriate, he has created new ones.

Stage IV

As the decade turned to 1970, Clark was named Distinguished University Professor at City College of the City University of New York. This appointment propelled his career into stage IV. In addition to this recognition, his professional peers in the American Psychological Association elected him to the presidency of that organization in 1970–1971, when he was fifty-six years old. In 1978, when he was sixty-four, he received the first Distinguished Contributions to Psychology in the Public Interest Award. Kenneth Clark took early retirement from the City University in 1975, when he was sixty-one years old, after spending thirty-three years at that post. Upon retirement he was awarded emeritus status as Distinguished University Professor.

Clark continues to serve on the New York State Board of Regents, continues to publish—*Pathos of Power* (1974) is his most recent book—and continues his public-affairs and community-service activities. As a vehicle for these, he organized a family-consulting firm of which he is president. Clark, Phipps, Clark, and Harris, Inc., is a firm that provides professional consultation on personnel matters, with emphasis on human-relations, race-relations, and affirmative-action programs. At the age of sixty-seven, Clark was still going strong in a "career as a social scientist that has been devoted to translating principles of human behavior into policies and programs that improve the quality of life for the poor and disadvantaged" (Evans 1980, p.63).

PERSONAL CHARACTERISTICS

Kenneth Clark, a man of strong opinions, is unafraid of conflict. Yet he is a kind person with a sense of humor, one who empathizes with the poor and the powerless.

Commitment, morality, and *ethics* are words that flavor his conversations. He can give love; but equally important, he knows how to receive love and to depend gracefully on others. He is full of praise for his mother and his wife as strong people on whom he has depended and who have been supportive of him. Clark believes that it takes courage both to give and to receive love.

Clark acknowledges that in his unyielding quest for quality and equality there probably are inconsistencies and even rigidities in some of his ideas. He comes to terms with these frailties through his own sense of humor, which, to him, is the leavening that reflects a perspective beyond narrow, egocentric preoccupations.

Kenneth Clark is an involved social psychologist who believes that issues of justice and power are central in social science research. He is a social psychologist who knows which side he is on.

ANALYTIC SUMMARY

The two most meaningful stages in kinship system for Kenneth Clark were the periods (stages I and III) he spent in the family of orientation, which supported and sustained him through college and a portion of graduate school, and in the family of procreation, which took up almost where the family of orientation left off. Stage II, the transitional period of an independent householder, was of short duration. The dominant figure in his family of orientation was his mother. Clark calls his mother and his wife the key women in his life who have sustained and supported him. His marriage was a stabilizing force in his life for more than four decades.

Such stability and loyalty are characteristics of other dimensions of Clark's life. Clark began teaching at City College of the City University of New York when he was twenty-eight years old, and continued as a faculty member of the same institution for thirty-three years. He moved to New York with his family when he was four years old and has remained a resident of the New York City metropolitan area for sixty-three years. There is something stable and steady about Kenneth Clark that has sustained an unusual career of scholarship, public affairs, and community service.

His educational career was completed without interruption. Graduating from high school at the age of sixteen and completing stages I and II in education, Clark had a head start on stages III and IV, college and graduate school. He breezed through these stages in six years, moving directly to the next stage after completing an earlier one. His marriage—stage III in the kinship system—did not take place until after he completed college and had commenced stage IV in education, graduate school. He was halfway through graduate school when he married. It is interesting that marriage was postponed until he was deep into the graduate studies of stage IV, since Clark had known his future wife since the college years of stage II.

Having married and completed his graduate education by the age of twenty-six, Clark was ready to begin his professional career. He made a few false starts that did not work out to satisfaction. These must have been a bit unsettling and may have contributed to the length of his stay at City College, since he found it to be a supportive setting.

At the age of twenty-eight and following his appointment to City College as a psychology instructor, Clark's career unfolded through four stages of almost equal lengths ranging from eight to eleven years. The eight years in stage I was needed to accommodate Clark's community-service activities in addition to his teaching, researching, and writing. Indeed, there is some indication that the community service impeded scholarly writing, but only in a modest way. Stage II lasted for nine years and involved teaching, research, writing, and public service. To this heavy commitment was added public service which was a consuming responsibility until the U.S. Supreme Court rendered its 1954 decision on school desegregation. It was Clark's participation in the school-desegregation case that greatly enhanced his total career and propelled him into stage III, which consolidated skills developed earlier and accommodated new skills developed in administration. Stage III also was the period when some public honors were bestowed and responsibility for the leadership of a learned society was assumed. This stage, which began when Clark was forty-five years old, lasted over a decade; it witnessed a tremendous increase in Clark's scholarly writings.

Stage IV was similar to the preceding stage, except that the public honors were more prestigious and the positions to which Clark was elevated involved more extensive responsibilities. So extensive were Clark's commitments before and during this stage that something had to give as he approached the sixth decade of his life. During this period he reduced his teaching, taking early retirement at the age of sixty-one; but he increased his community-service and administrative activities through the organization of a family-consulting firm.

In summary, the career of Kenneth Clark has been one in which academic affairs and public affairs have complemented each other. Blending these two together so well has been one of his major contributions as a psychologist.

CHAPTER 5

A Political Scientist Who Cares about the Ordinary

Matthew Holden, Jr.

A DISTINGUISHED POLITICAL SCIENTIST who has focused on comparative politics and international relations, urban planning, and policy analysis, Matthew Holden, Jr., has been critical of the professionals in his field for not giving attention to domestic issues as well as to foreign policy. Foreign-policy analysis is a long-standing tradition in political science, but domestic-policy study is not (Holden and Dresang 1975 p. 12). In an essay appropriately titled "On the Misunderstanding of Important Phenomena," Holden observed that "the tumults of Boston, Cincinnati, Dayton, St. Petersberg, and Tampa are pushed off Page One by the more dramatically dangerous confrontation of Jew and Arab . . . .But every sign is that they will yet return to the nation's consciousness." In a real sense, Holden said, one could call the domestic tumults "the most genuine type of maximum feasible participation of the poor . . . or the ringing once more of Mr. Jefferson's fire bell" (Holden, 1968:111).

A PROFESSIONAL POLICYMAKER

Political scientist Stuart Nagel of the University of Illinois has noted "a substantial change," a "new orientation" among political scientists "within the last few years." Political scientists are beginning to apply the scientific method to the study of problems that have broad significance on the domestic scene. Nagel attributes this change to many sources, including the civil rights movement. In his judgment, "policy studies is the most rapidly developing field within political science" (Nagel 1975, pp.7–8).

Matthew Holden, Jr., is at the forefront of this trust among political scientists, as manifested by the themes examined in his publications and the nature of his public-service participation. Holden not only writes about the politics of bureaucracy and administration but also has had extensive personal experience in public-administration research and as a policymaking practitioner at federal, state, and local levels.

His practical experience in public-administration research dates back to the late 1950s, when Holden joined the staffs of the Cleveland Metropolitan Service Commission and the Cuyahoga County Charter Commission. These local experiences in public-administration research were reinforced and refined later by appointments in state and federal government. In 1977 Holden received a presidential appointment as commissioner of the Federal Energy Regulatory Commission, U.S. Department of Energy. The Federal Regulatory Commission is an updated version of the old Federal Power Commission that was formed in the 1920s. Holden has supplemented his experience of about a decade in public-administration research and public policymaking with about two decades of work as a professor on university faculties. Matthew Holden, Jr., then, unites both the theoretical and the practical. He is a political scientist who has made a difference because of the legal authority behind his official actions and the logical and perceptive analyses presented in his published works.

That his peers had cast more votes for him than for other political scientists in our survey of outstanding black professionals was a surprise to Holden, who believed that his serious scholarly writings were of "limited scope, substance, and depth." Holden's full-time function in recent years as a professional policymaker has been, in his words, "highly beneficial to me from an intellectual point of view." However, he is reluctant to be counted among the outstanding because he finds it hard to believe that his work measures up to the "truly remarkable academic writings" of scholars such as Ralph Bunche. Others, however, had a different view.

In our study, more scholars were nominated as outstanding in political science than in any of the other disciplines investigated. This fact probably indicates what Holden himself humorously called "the fratricidal (but non-lethal) war of the discipline," particularly the divisions between behavioral and normative political science (Holden 1966, p.2). Because of the great division in the field, when we sought nominations of outstanding black political scientists, five received multiple nominations. This rather large panel (we anticipated that the number would be not greater than three) was submitted to a nationwide sample of eighty-seven political scientists, both black and white, of whom sixty-eight participated in the study by ranking the panel members. A majority opinion was not expected, given the relatively large panel of nominees ranked by a relatively small sample. A decisive plurality of twenty-one political scientists of all races and in all regions of the country said that Matthew Holden, Jr., was the most outstanding. All others received fewer votes. The absence of overwhelming consensus by a majority on the most outstanding black political scientist reflects as much the discipline and the diversity of interests within it as it does the age of the scholars nominated. None had retired and finished his or her career.

Holden is a widely read scholar in many different social science fields, including history, sociology, and anthropology. He has conducted several important investigations in the areas of policy studies, political decision making, and urban planning; he has written or edited several books, chapters of books, monographs, and journal articles.

Beyond the fact that more than a third of his career has been spent working full time in the application of principle to practice, Holden was surprised that a substantial number of his colleagues recognized his contributions because, in his words, "my work always seems to be moving in the other direction than the work of some in political science." He said that he refuses to be bound by the concepts in his field and that he has never been excessively respectful of received doctrines of what the discipline is: "One has to go ahead and do what one genuinely wants to do."

What Holden has not realized is that his work has been ahead of his field, and not out of the mainstream. Holden has served on the council of the Policy Studies Organization. In 1975 Sage Publications brought out the first volume of its *Yearbook of Politics and Public Policy*. Holden was the senior coeditor of that volume. In 1972, Holden was chairman of the Section on Policy Analysis of the American Political Science Association. Thus Holden was present at the creation of this renewed interest in policy analysis, which, with his customary manner of understatement, he prefers to call "the revival of policy studies" (Holden and Dresang 1975, p.10).

In general, Holden sees himself as an ordinary professional using his own experience to help him become more knowledgeable of the process in decision making (Holden 1966, pp.44–45) and of the ways of achieving the twin goals of "social equalization" and "social peace" (Holden 1971, pp.64–65). For this reason, Holden makes a strong case for the "relevance of ordinary experience" as a guide for professional action. He asked this question of the scholars who might challenge him because of his known bias toward perception and interpretation of ordinary experience: "[How many] would accurately predict their own behaviors as consultants, teachers, deans, etc. . . . if they accepted only that evidence susceptible to the kind of verification demanded in much of the formal theory?" (Holden 1966, p.6).

While making the case for the use of ordinary experience in the analysis of public policy, Holden has developed, in passing, a unique and extra ordinary idea—that of urban statehood (Holden 1971, p.70). This demonstrates the fertile mind of Matthew Holden, Jr., and his capacity to embrace bold concepts. Yet Holden would dismiss such praise as unwarranted because, in his words, "the idea has actually floated about in textbook form for many years" and simply has been neglected (Holden 1971, p.71).

Holden's urban-statehood idea is a way of introducing cultural pluralism into the federal bureaucracy. When the number of blacks and other racial minorities in the decision-making structure constitutes a sufficiently large critical mass, federal officials will identify issues of race relations as important and will develop strategic objectives and timetables to resolve them, said Holden, who belives that decentralization leads away from rather than toward black power. His idea is that any urban unit that has a population greater than that of Arizona, Alaska, or Hawaii can become a new state and can participate in the mainstream with an autonomous base of power. If a minimum arbitrary figure of 500,000 people were used, this would result in twenty-one additional states, to make a total of seventy-one United States. Probably ten or more of the twenty-one new city-states would be more or less under black control. Such areas would be electing not merely mayors with limited power, according to Holden, but also members of the U.S. House and Senate. [Twenty] senators bound by a common interest and a common necessity are a bloc likely to carry great weight, which is precisely the purpose of the proposal" (Holden 1971, pp.70–71).

The urban-statehood proposal, as reported by Holden, was sketched because it is unusual and because it illustrates the quality of Holden's mind in developing a political design. One can think clearly and daringly, as Holden does, only if one is free of egocentric preoccupation. Holden is a humble man, but not mild-mannered. Indeed, he is very assertive, as indicated by the announcement of his statehood proposal and as further discussion of his identification with others will reveal. Holden is an interesting combination of contrasting characteristics not unlike those of the contrasting communities in which he grew up in Mound Bayou, Mississippi, and Chicago, Illinois.

FAMILY BACKGROUND

Childhood in Mound Bayou

Matthew Holden lived in Mound Bayou, Mississippi, until he was thirteen years old. Then his family moved to Chicago. He described Mound Bayou, an all-black town settled by ex-slaves from the Jefferson Davis plantation, as a place where there was great pride. One of the founders of the town survived until 1924, just seven years before Holden was born. Thus in his early childhood years Holden heard stories about the early settlers. Holden said that Isaiah T. Montgomery, one of Mound Bayou's founders, had two basic themes in his philosophy: "If you haven't got power yourself, keep powerful friends," and "The survival of black people depends on being able to do something on their own." Holden said that many people, both black and white, respected Isaiah Montgomery. According to Holden, Montgomery was a "tough-minded man" who also was "roundly denounced, with good reason, for having made the decision to support the Constitution of 1890 in Mississippi."

One of Holden's grandfathers was a preacher who served four different churches, visting one each month. Before his death at the age of fifty-three, he had accumulated in Amite County, Mississippi, "a good deal of land, about 560 acres," according to Holden. Later, Holden's family moved to Bolivar County. The family worked the land, with Holden who was born in Mound Bayou of Bolivar County taking his turn in the field, chopping and picking cotton. Holden said, however, that his field work always was done after school hours.

Of his extended kinship system, including the Holdens, the Welch family (his maternal grandfather's people), and the Canedy-Clark tribe (his maternal grandmother's people), Holden said "there were several elements of my family that had seen, in the family mythology, better days. And, on all sides, we thought of ourselves as eminently substantial and respectable people." Holden described "a sense of uprightness and of being somebody which went with owning a little piece of land or sometimes a sizable piece of land." That sense of uprightness associated with ownership of property, Holden said, "was extremely important."

Holden's family insisted that he go to school. Illness was the only legitimate excuse for staying at home. His family never kept him out of school so that he could help them in the field, not even at harvest time. Holden put it this way: "My father was insistent that I, his son, go to school There was great emphasis on education in my family. School was important to me and my family."

Holden's father had completed five years of school, and his mother had finished the eleventh grade of high school. Their jobs when they left the farm were in service or laboring occupations and semiskilled work, but they wanted their offspring to achieve more. Going to college, said Holden, was as preordained as anything could be: "Do you eat when you get hungry? That is how preordained college was for me."

Holden was not the first in the family to go to college. He had an uncle, his father's brother, whom everyone described as smart. The family wanted him to be a doctor and sent him to Alcorn College in Mississippi, but the uncle died before finishing Alcorn. "The family had their hopes pinned on him." When Holden came along everyone thought he was very much like his uncle Samuel: "This is how their hope and ambition centered on me."

Holden had two half-brothers and grew up around many relatives. In the household formed by the marriage of his mother and father, however, he was in effect an only child. The ambitions and unfulfilled wishes of his parents, especially his mother, centered on him too.

Holden describes his mother as "an extremely intelligent woman," who continues to read the newspaper and the Bible, who owns a copy of everything he has written, and who is proud of his work. His mother's ambition had been to graduate from high school and go to Rust College in Mississippi. When a woman in the community offered to pay for Holden's mother's college expenses, however, her father, not wishing to be obligated to the giver, would not accept the offer. Later, Holden said, his grandfather "confessed to his daughter" that he did her a great injustice by not letting her go to college.

The drought was severe. The crops failed. There was no alternative but to pull up stakes and seek opportunity elsewhere. It was 1944, when wartime production beckoned blacks to northern cities. Holden's family went to Chicago, where his parents found work. Holden had passed his thirteenth birthday.

Adolescence and Young Adulthood in Chicago

It was in Chicago that Holden's interest in politics was awakened: "I hung around my father and uncle and listened to the ward committeeman as he talked to them. Instead of playing with the kids, I stood around and heard him discuss politics. Sitting around ward headquarters in Chicago, I heard things. I was young and no threat, so the ward committeeman, William Dawson, talked with me. He was an extraordinary person, a man of *realpolitik*, a supreme pragmatist, a genius." To this day Holden greatly respects Congressman William Dawson: "He was a good platform orator and a rough back-alley fighter."

Describing his own manner, Holden indicated that some of the rough-and-tumble of Chicago precinct politics and the determination of an all-black farming community in Mississippi have remained with him: "I have always been probably a little more assertive than most people. But when I was a teenager, I was subject to as many doubts as anyone. I could walk by a door four times when looking for a job before I had enough courage to open the door and go in." Despite his doubts, "I also believe that you should go after the chance." For example, "Once someone tells you that you can't do something, then that is what you have to do." Because of this philosophy of life, "I doubt that I had mentors. There were people who influenced me. One, in particular, was Norton Long. The man's mind is a field of electricity; it was he, more than anyone else, whom I sought to emulate in maintaining knowledge and interests across a wide area and to relate things across a wide area. St. Clair Drake—a smart and kind person of great integrity—was another profound source of influence as was Melville Herskovits and, at far distance, Judge William Hastie and the mythology of Grandfather William Holden, a mover and shaker."

One person Holden could always count on was his mother, who nurtured him through the doubting years of adolescence and provided a safe and secure shelter to which he could return after his probes into the outside world. After the move to Chicago, Holden's mother and father eventually separated. Holden remained a member of his mother's household until he had received a master's degree and was drafted into the U.S army.

Thereafter he would spend time in the army and in Cleveland, Evanston, and Detroit, pursuing graduate study and work. During this period, which lasted eight years, he was an independent householder until he married Dorothy Amanda Howard when he was thirty-two years old. They have two children.

EDUCATION

College

Holden attended two different colleges, the University of Chicago and then Roosevelt University, from which he received his bachelor's degree.

At the age of sixteen he enrolled in the University of Chicago and remained there off and on for about four years, but he made little progress toward completing a degree. In 1946 the University of Chicago was experimenting with various methods of instruction. The institution offered numerous options and imposed few external limits. One experiment involved eliminating the requirement that students attend classes. Holden experienced the University of Chicago as a learning environment of two extremes—"a combination of freedom and rigid structure." All this had a negative effect on his grades, and eventually he withdrew. Holden described his University of Chicago experience as "truly great and beneficial." There he learned a great deal, "including an attitude about learning." Nevertheless, he "flunked out" because, in his words, "I was unable to muster the self-discipline to cope with both the intellectual opportunity and the intellectual freedom, as well as to overcome my own timidity."

Roosevelt University in Chicago was a good setting for Holden after he left the University of Chicago. When he attended college, "there were no special privileges for me." Holden attended Roosevelt two years, from 1950 to 1952. Intending to go into law, he majored in political science and took a minor in history. At the time of his graduation, however, he realized that his entire undergraduate record was not good enough to get him admitted to the kind of law school he wanted to attend. Therefore, he decided to pursue graduate study in political science. Holden's decision to go into political science also can be interpreted as an extension of his childhood conversations with the ward committeeman and the interest in political matters these experiences awakened in him.

Graduate School

Despite his stop-and-go performance in college, Holden completed his undergraduate education the year he turned twenty-one. The next year he enrolled in Northwestern University in Evanston, Illinois, a suburb of Chicago. He obtained his master's degree in political science two years later.

With the first level of graduate education behind him, Holden's plan was to join the Foreign Service and become a career officer. He crammed for the examination, passed it, and became a candidate. When he was twenty-four years old, however, he was called into military service for two years. The Foreign Service deferred final decision on his appointment since he had not yet passed the language examination.

Getting out of the army, where he attained the rank of sergeant, Holden decided to continue his political science studies. He needed money to do this, however, so he decided to take a job to finance the last phase of his graduate education. At this point Holden was on his own, with limited funds and no sponsorship. He was making things happen, going after opportunity. He took the public-administration examination, passed it, and secured jobs first with the Cleveland Metropolitan Commission and then with the Charter Commission in Cuyahoga County.

Holden returned to Northwestern University in 1958 and three years later obtained his Ph.D. degree at the age of twenty-nine. Even with these interruptions, Holden was able to complete his graduate studies nine years after receiving his bachelor's degree. He supported himself during this period by working at the Charter Commission, teaching in the evening division of Northwestern University, and working as a research assistant at the University of Illinois, Institute of Government and Public Affairs. The advice that Holden often gives to others, he accepted for himself during this period in his life. He believes that "one has to invest a good deal of oneself and one's own resources in one's professional development and not rely solely on resources that come by subsidy." Holden did precisely this. He crammed a great deal of activity and effort into three short years and was ready to commence his career as a scholar in 1961.

CAREER

Stage I

Holden interrupted his graduate studies once for military service and again for full-time employment. Fortunately, his work represented an application of his professional interest.

From 1957 through 1959 Holden served on the staffs of the Cleveland Metropolitan Service Commission and the Cuyahoga Charter Commission as research assistant and staff consultant, respectively. Although these were entry-level appointments, they provided enormous practical experience that sparked Holden's theoretical interest in urban politics and gave him insight into cities. These jobs appropriately should be classified as stage I in Holden's career. They provided practical experience in urban planning and opportunities to get experience in research and writing. Holden prepared two important monographs during this period, *County Government in Ohio* (1958a) and *Intergovernmental Agreements in the Cleveland Metropolitan Area* (1958b). Stage I lasted a total of four years.

Stage II

Upon receipt of the Ph.D. degree, Holden was appointed instructor and later assistant professor in the Department of Political Science at Michigan's Wayne State University in 1961. This appointment began stage II in Holden's professional career, which lasted eight years and included an appointment at the University of Pittsburgh beginning in 1963. Holden was twenty-nine years old when he obtained his first full-time teaching appointment.

Holden had always wanted to be a professor. He had concluded that college teaching "was an occupation with the least racial

impedimenta." In his longstanding practice of seizing on opportunity, Holden decided to secure the necessary credentials to become
a college professor. Holden was appointed to a university faculty
during the summer session of 1960. He had to work hard to catch up
since stage I had not involved full-time teaching. During this period,
he taught at both Wayne State University and the University of
Pittsburgh, did research, and began a distinguished career of writing
for learned journals.

No books were written during stage II, but eleven articles and
monographs on a range of subjects were published—an average of
more than one a year for the entire period. One of Holden's favorite
articles, published in 1963, the year he moved to Pittsburgh for a
duration of three years, was entitled "Litigation and the Political
Order." It appeared in the *Western Political Quarterly* (Holden 1963)
and discusses litigation as a form of social combat, insurrection
without arms.

Holden served as a consultant to Resources for the Future during
the summers of 1965 and 1966. On the basis of these experiences, he
prepared a magnificent essay on regulatory decision making that
established him as a major theoretician on the politics of decision
making. The particular theme of the essay was pollution control.
Holden took a major public-policy problem and demonstrated how
analysis of it was one of the most important ways for determining
deficiencies of decision-making analysis (Holden 1966, p.4).

During this stage of his career, Holden acted on the advice he
had received from Norton Long in graduate school. He was taking
particular problems and finding common principles within them.
This approach to political science, he said, helped him "to see
general principles in particular knowledge . . . of international relations and cities and helped . . . to overcome compartmentaliz-
ation." Holden was at his best implementing this approach in the
review essays that he prepared for professional journals. He could
take half a dozen different books on a common topic such as law
enforcement or race relations, find common principles running
through them, and present a critique of the books individually and
collectively that in the end would contribute to political science
theory.

A general deficiency of social scientists that he found and
reported in one of his essays, entitled "Judgment and the Right
Questions," is that they tend to be afflicted with parochialism of
time." (Holden 1973). They fail to recognize the meaning of
change—"that the parameters within which capacity is to be mea-
sured are different, for the same population, from one time to
another" (Holden 1966, p.117).

Holden stated that "the most important problems in social
science, in this generation, still are problems of discovery, rather than
problems of verification." He believes that verification is crucial, but

that it is with respect to discovery "that we still have important problems with which to deal." Holden states that this is his orientation probably because his "intellectual foundations owe more to Aristotle, the Old Testament, and Hobbs than to the Enlightenment and Marx."

Holden's reputation was growing. He was becoming known in the field by his writings and by his participation in numerous symposia. By the time stage II had ended, Holden had caught up with some and surpassed others in his writing. During this period he published in such prestigious journals as *Midwest Journal of Political Science, Western Political Quarterly, Urban Affairs Quarterly,* and *American Political Science Review.* During the eight-year period of stage II, Holden established himself as a serious scholar.

Stage III

Stage III in his career began when Holden was thirty-eight years old. In 1969 the University of Wisconsin at Madison invited him to join its faculty as a full professor in the Department of Political Science. For years this department has ranked among the top ten in political science in the nation. The same year that Holden moved to Wisconsin, he was elected to the board of directors of the Social Science Research Council. Later he would accept appointment as a member of the Assembly of Behavioral and Social Sciences of the National Academy of Science. These appointments indicate the respect with which he was regarded by his peers.

Holden served as an elected member of the Council of the American Political Science Association from 1972 to 1974 and as chairman of its Section on Policy Analysis the first year of his term on the Council. In 1973 he served a term as council member of the Policy Studies Organization; in 1976–1977 he was elected vice-president of the American Political Science Association. Meanwhile, he worked with the regional organization, the Midwest Political Science Association, and was an active participant in the local Wisconsin Capital Chapter of the American Society for Public Administration. When asked how the careers of other blacks in political science might be enhanced, Holden said, "One has to be willing to invest the time and effort to participate in the full range of the activities of the scholars of the discipline and not withdraw from them." This approach has worked for Holden, and he predicts that it will work for others. Holden has moved toward the front of his discipline by assuming responsibilities of service in its associations.

Meanwhile his other contributions to political science and public policymaking have escalated. Holden wrote or edited six books during this period and increased his participation in public affairs. He served on the Governor's Committee on Metropolitan Area

Problems in Wisconsin; as a consultant to several federal agencies, such as the Department of Housing and Urban Development; and as a member of the Air Quality Advisory Board.

Most of all, Holden increased his policymaking skills during the third stage of his political science career. In 1975 he left the university to become commissioner of the Wisconsin Public Service Commission. Two years later, he came to Washington, D.C., to be sworn in as Commissioner of the Federal Energy Regulatory Commission.

Stage III of Holden's career has been fruitful. During this period, which began in 1969, he has refined his teaching skills, continued his research, increased his writing, participated in public and professional affairs, and developed new skills at state and national levels in public policymaking. Holden closed out stage III in his career when his term as federal commissioner expired and began Stage IV with appointment as the Henry L. and Grace M. Doherty Professor of Government and Foreign Affairs at the University of Virginia in 1981 at the age of 50.

PERSONAL CHARACTERISTICS

Holden is assertive, blunt, honest, and shy. These characteristics are combined in a person who is at once skeptical and kind. He is energetic and enormously talented. Once Holden takes a stand, there is no confusion about what it is. He is direct and decisive in articulating his views. He is respectful of people, kind in evaluating their professional work, always fair in his criticism. He may question or even denounce ideas but never the individual who utters or writes them.

Because he has followed a philosophy of life of self-direction and professional competitiveness, Holden has said that personally he has not experienced racial discrimination in his academic career in a form and to an extent that was decisive, except perhaps when he began to entertain thoughts of opportunities for the administrative side of his career. In other words, Holden said, "I don't have a perception of having been seriously impeded by being black, and in some ways being black may have given me an extra vision." From this perspective, he said, "Maybe being black was even a *practical* asset."

Concerning his assertiveness, he said that he had to make it clear that no one has a right to exclude him. For example, "I made an issue out of living in the rooming houses near the Northwestern campus when no blacks lived in the houses because I would not accept the concept that others had a right to exclude me."

The real issue, said Holden, especially for black professional political scientists, is to find ways to incorporate discomfort and adversity into focused activity: "One must confront issues of survival in a world of power on the predicate that the world will not cease to be a world of power but that justice is likely to be lasting when it is achieved and enforced with knowledge of the use of power." Finally, he said, "The presence or absence of knowledge of how to deal with power will determine whether or not the world will drive you up the wall."

ANALYTIC SUMMARY

This summary of the career of Matthew Holden, Jr., will demonstrate linkages between family, education, and work. Of particular interest are the various stages in each of these processes, the events that interconnect a stage within a system and those that interrelate different systems to each other.

Holden, indeed, had not just a family but an extended kinship system in his early childhood in Mississippi. There were plenty of aunts, uncles, cousins, and grandparents. A farming family of limited means never had enough resources to give similar opportunities to every member. Thus there was a tendency to pin hope on the family member who was believed to be smart, and to rally around and support the forward movement of that individual by providing more schooling. Family members sublimated the fulfillment of their personal ambitions through the achievements of the chosen one. In his early years Holden was identified by his family as the smart one. He was like his uncle, who had died before completing college and becoming a doctor as the family had hoped he would. Holden's kinship system and his family of orientation nurtured and sustained him through childhood, adolescence, and young adulthood. He remained a member of his mother's household until he received a master's degree.

Despite Holden's difficulties in applying himself diligently to his college studies during late adolescence, his family of orientation never gave up on him. His parents supported him through six years of formal study in college and involved him in informal learning experiences such as the trips he made with his father and uncle to the office of the ward committeeman. Regardless of how difficult the problems that confronted him, Holden always knew he had the support of his family of orientation behind him. And this made a difference.

After a two-year stint in military service, Holden had to make it more or less on his own. His parents were blue-collar workers with limited education who found employment in laboring, service, or semiskilled occupations. There was bread enough in his mother's household, but little of anything else to share.

So that he might work and study, and study and work, and still complete the stage of graduate education by the age of thirty (despite the interruption of military service), Holden shuttled back and forth between entry-level jobs in public administration and school, holding some of these jobs coterminously with graduate school matriculation.

Holden was able to do this because he had no family obligations. He remained an independent householder eight years. He was two years into the second stage of his career before he married at the age of thirty-two. It appears that Holden waited until he achieved the occupation of his choice before taking on the responsibilities of stage III in the kinship system—the family of procreation. At the time of this study Matthew and Dorothy Holden had been married eighteen years.

With reference to education, clearly the hope and aspiration that Holden's family had for him must have had a motivating effect. His struggles to get an education were his own, but they were also for a family who in part fulfilled their own ambitions through his success. He breezed through the early stages of his education and graduated from high school at the age of sixteen.

Holden may have been ready for college, but not for the first college in which he enrolled. Although he spent six years in college rather than the customary four, it should be noted that Holden did not drop out. Too many people had their hopes and ambitions pinned on him for him to stop because of a few difficulties. Although he entered the college stage of his career in mid-adolescence, Holden did not complete his graduate education until the age of twenty-nine. This fact has two implications—first that those who start early do not always end early; second, that a later ending of one's education does not necessarily hamper an effective beginning of a professional career. Perhaps one may have to cram more activities into one stage of a career that could have been better distributed among all stages. One can call the overloading in one stage in one system because of the excessive length of a development stage in another system a form of compensation.

One way that Holden compensated for the extended state of graduate education, and the need to begin his career outside his chosen occupation before the completion of graduate school, was to remain single for an extended period. The period of an independent householder, which often is a transition period of short duration, was an eight-year stage in Holden's life. This period gave him the flexibility to accommodate career and education objectives until they could be brought into harmony with each other.

Throughout all the stages and within all the systems, one sees major events that affected the course of Holden's life: the move to Chicago in the family system, the interruption of his education by military service, his move to the University of Wisconsin. These and other events linked family, education, and career, and the various stages within each system.

The unfolding events in Holden's life is an interesting mixture of both seizing the chance and waiting for the opportunity.

CHAPTER 6

An Objective and Sympathetic Literary Critic

Darwin T. Turner

DARWIN THEODORE TROY TURNER-the alliterative character of his name is indicative of the artistic signs and symbols that have surrounded him from the start. He was born in Cincinnati, Ohio, in 1931, during the depths of the Depression. Some have called the city of his birth the gateway to the North; others have dubbed it the northernmost southern city. The setting of his childhood and youth, then, was a place betwixt and between.

LITERATURE AND THE BLACK EXPERIENCE

If art flourishes when science falters, Turner was born at a time when art was needed for hope, for the science-based economy of U.S. society had crumbled. Beyond this, Turner's childhood occurred in a period when the United States was at war. Anyone, particularly a sensitive young person, would want to know what this meant. The art of words was Turner's vehicle for making sense out of the world, its people, and his place in life. As stated by Jean Toomer, "art is devoted to life" (Turner 1971a, p.124). Turner has dedicated himself to understanding the art of writing and, consequently, the substance of life.

All words and combinations of words have interested Turner over the years. Essays, fiction, poetry, and drama have attracted his critical concern (Turner 1970). His role as a critic has been outstanding because he strives to be objective. Turner is a critic who writes objectively about black authors because that is the group with which he is most familiar (Turner, 1968, p.690). He writes about black authors as a way of "helping to recall some from semioblivion" (Moore 1971, p.ix). Finally, Turner writes about black authors as a way of understanding the United States. "As Americans," he says, "they respond to issues which touch all Americans" (Turner 1968, p.687). Reflecting his range of interest in humanity, Turner also writes about white authors.

Turner sees the American experience manifested in the black experience. Others have come to this conclusion as well. In his book *Black Fiction* Roger Rosenblatt writes, "Themes which have been ascribed as characteristically American . . . are the themes of black fiction as well . . . the problem of national self-definition which has regularly dominated American writers is at the heart of black fiction." American literary conventions, Rosenblatt said, have provided black writers "something to lean on and push against at the same time" (Rosenblatt 1974, p.4–5). Corroborating this idea, Turner says of black essayists: "[They] came of age, then rejected the age." Nevertheless, "their ideas have meaning for American readers" (Turner 1970, p.8).

Turner has had a fruitful career appraising the works both of black and of other scholars. In the words of Harry Moore of Southern Illinois University, Darwin Turner presents an "indepth . . . sympathetic analysis," "a fuller comprehension," with the "gifts of understanding" (Moore 1971, pp. ix–x). His appraisals also are objective and honest. J. Corene Elam has call Turner's assessments "meticulous" and "concise." As a scholar, Elam says, Turner is a trail-blazer, especially in the way he has handled materials that fully reintroduced Jean Toomer to the American reading public. Darwin Turner is at his best in analyzing the intellectual and psychological development of authors (Elam 1981, p.56).

Turner has written excellent scholarly appraisals of the work of others but has not produced a large body of artistic work of his own other than a volume of poetry (Turner 1964).

As far back as his college years, Turner always has had dual concerns that have competed with each other, blurring the focus of his career. These dual concerns and the energy required to resolve them may have affected his creative thrust. He enrolled in the University of Cincinnati when he was only thirteen. Rather than lengthening the period of early study for the purpose of discovering vocational interests, as he could have done without adversely affecting his future, Turner completed his college career in three rather than the customary four years. Turner's undergraduate major was English, but he seriously considered mathematics; yet he always wanted to be an actor. Turner applied to several law schools for postgraduate study, but accepted a scholarship to enroll in a master's degree program in English. He had no intention of teaching, but his first job was in education, as have been his subsequent and current appointments. Immediately after receiving his first-level graduate degree, Turner got married and found a job, although his family and particularly his grandmother preferred that he go on then to earn a doctoral degree. After two years of teaching, Turner resigned his first job, went to Chicago, and enrolled in the University of Chicago to study for the doctorate.

Turner has always been interested in research and writing. His first short story was published while he was still a graduate student, although he was also a full-time teacher. For about two decades, however, his career in higher education was split, with joint responsibilities in administration, on the one hand, and teaching and research on the other. In the area of ideas, Turner also exhibits contrasting themes that may conflict with each other.

With these contradictions to overcome, it is remarkable that Turner has made such extensive contributions. During a thirty-two-year career that began in 1949, he has written or edited approximately seventeen books and forty-eight articles, averaging more than one article a year and one book every two years. He has critically appraised the work of both black and white authors. Currently he is in charge of the Afro-American Studies Program at the University of Iowa, Iowa City and is also University of Iowa Foundation Distinguished Professor of English. The English department at that university has ranked consistently among the top third of all English departments in the nation.

Turner not only has been a creative critic, but also has developed the tools of his trade and shared them with others so that they might pursue their work with greater ease. Seldom is one honored for doing the support work for a discipline. Turner, undertaking such a responsibility, has published *A Guide to Composition* (1960), *Standards for Freshman Composition* (1961), *Afro-American Writers: A Bibliography* (1970), and *Syllabus for Afro-American Literature* (1981). He did all this while also writing or editing scholarly books and writing articles for learned journals. Moreover, he has been a good citizen of his discipline and has served as president of one of its learned associations and on several committees of professional organizations. All this has been accomplished during three stages of Turner's career. The final stage has yet to begin.

FAMILY BACKGROUND

Turner's intellectual gifts flow naturally from his family, who nurtured his sense of self-worth and self-esteem. One of his books is dedicated "To my Grandmother who was proud and to Mother and Dad who are." This dedicatory page indicates the nature of the context from which he came.

Turner's paternal grandfather was a college teacher and a public school principal. He had a long career in education and was honored by the St. Louis public school system, which named a building after him. Turner remarked, "Everyone says I'm like my grandfather." His grandfather was the first black male to graduate from the University of Chicago, where he earned a Ph.D. in biology summa cum laude. He was a prolific writer and an editor, who specialized in the study of ants and bees. Turner said his grandfather was "a great inspiration" to him.

On his mother's side of the family, Turner described his grandmother as "the driving force . . . a determined woman." His grandmother, he said, "valued people according to their intellect." She came from a line of educators. Her grandfather, Owen Nickens, (Turner's maternal great great-grandfather) was one of the first black teachers in Cincinnati. According to Turner, Nickens founded the first successful school for blacks in that city. Turner's grandmother obtained the master's degree the same year that her daughter, Turner's mother, received a graduate degree. At eighteen, his mother was the youngest graduate in the history of the University of Cincinnati at the time she received her baccalaureate degree. She received both a Bachelor of Arts and a Bachelor of Science in Education degree and obtained a Master of Arts degree in English as well as a Master of Science in Education degree. Turner's mother was an English teacher in the public school system.

Turner's father studied chemistry and took graduate courses at the University of Cincinnati, but he did not finish his dissertation because he feared that obtaining a Ph.D. would persuade him to teach. After working as a research chemist, he studied pharmacy at the University of Illinois and received a graduate degree in that field.

For business reasons, Turner's father preferred Chicago, where he operated three drugstores. His mother moved there at first but later returned to Cincinnati, which she preferred. However, she would go back to Chicago often to visit with her husband. There were two children in Turner's family of orientation—Darwin and a younger brother, Charles, who eventually graduated from Harvard. The children remained in Cincinnati with their mother and her extended family.

EDUCATION

Turner said, "In my family, it was assumed that we would go to college if we wanted to. The money was available and the tradition

was there." Before college, however, there was public school education, which Turner moved through with dispatch. He was considered by many to be a prodigy and, indeed, was a subject in a
study of black precocious children that was undertaken by the
president of a black college a few decades ago. He entered public
school when he was four years old.

Turner enjoyed school at all levels. In high school, feeling that
his age mates were too young, he tended to associate with older
students. In college, he said, "I did the usual things that other
students did: I could play poker, pool, Ping-Pong; I spent hours
seeing movies and playing bridge."

Turner's mother and grandmother encouraged him in elementary school. They doted on him—the first new child in the family in
twenty-two years. Much of his education in the home during his
younger years, however, was provided by an older couple and an
aunt-in-law who babysat with him. Turner said, "Although I did
very well in the seventh and eighth grades, I had trouble in the ninth
grade when I transferred to the city's top academic high school, the
one that students entered only as a result of scores on standardized
tests." Turner's family hired a tutor to help him with ninth grade
algebra. In general, however, Turner said, "The family left me alone
rather than harassing me about studies."

He acknowledged that his family offered incentives at times. For
example, his grandmother offered him a dollar for every A he got
when he first enrolled in college. Even before he entered college, his
mother promised him a blue Buick convertible if he was elected to
Phi Beta Kappa. Amused by these promises, Turner recalled that he
got all A's the first term and later made Phi Beta Kappa, but never got
the dollars or the Buick until he bought one himself in later life.
There were several news stories about Turner's extraordinary mental
ability. As much as he could, Turner said, he tried to ignore all the
hoopla.

Primary and Secondary School Education

Turner enrolled in school when he was four years old and spent a
year in the first grade. On the recommendation of his teacher, he was
then skipped to the third grade. When he was six, he entered the
fourth grade, took a test, and was promoted to the sixth grade in
midyear. A news story about Turner at that time, which his wife has
preserved in a scrapbook, stated that he had the mental capacity of an
eleven-year old when he was only six. He finished all the years
normally required of high school students. Although he did not skip
any grades at the secondary level, he graduated from high school at
the age of thirteen because of his head start in elementary school and
the number of grades that he had skipped.

College and Graduate School

Because other members of Turner's family had attended the University of Cincinnati, that was where he enrolled. Having entered college at the age of thirteen, he was elected to Phi Beta Kappa at fifteen and received his B.A. at sixteen, his M.A. at eighteen, and his Ph.D. at twenty-five. His doctorate was earned at the University of Chicago. All the other higher-education degrees were received from Cincinnati.

In 1944, when he entered college, he found that people at the University of Cincinnati did not understand the black experience; but, he said, "I didn't worry about it when I was in college. I did the usual things and enjoyed my years at the University of Cincinnati." At the time, he said, "I didn't understand the black experience myself. I had led a sheltered, fortunate life—only occasionally experiencing the discrimination that harasses many young blacks."

Turner said that when he was young he saw Paul Robeson perform in Othello. Later Robeson became for him the image of a perfect man—an athlete, actor, and Phi Beta Kappa. After personally assessing the problems that blacks encountered in getting jobs in drama in those days, Turner said he decided against drama as a career, although he still wanted to be an actor when he was a college senior. Turner said a white director of drama at the University of Cincinnati offered to help get acting lessons for him if he wanted them. Even this staff member of the university who offered assistance, according to Turner, "questioned why any very intelligent person would want to be an actor." Turner said, "Looking back now, I doubt that I would have, because of limited opportunities." At any rate, by the time he received his M.A. degree, Turner said he had other more pressing interests: "I wanted to get married."

Turner's choice of English was precipitated by an advisor. Midway through his second year in college, his advisor told him that, because of the number of credits he had taken in the freshman year, the summer, and the fall term, he would be a junior at the beginning of the spring semester; therefore, he needed to choose a major. Turner said he continued to vascillate between mathematics and English in the short period when he was trying to decide. He also thought about majoring in astronomy, but English won: "I grew up with the Harvard Classics in our library at home. The works of Dickens were around. My mother had been in English. She was a teacher and my grandmother was a principal. Although I had no intention of teaching, I chose English when my advisor pushed me to pick a major."

Turner does not remember applying to the University of Cincinnati for graduate study in English. He does recall that upon completion of his undergraduate studies, he was offered a scholarship if he would agree to spend at least two years studying for an

M.A. degree in English. Turner applied to law school at Harvard, Yale, and Columbia, and was accepted at Columbia. When he received the scholarship from the University of Cincinnati, however, he decided to accept it. He still planned to go to law school but knew that, even after the three-year program, he would only be twenty-one, the minimum age for the bar.

At the age of eighteen, Turner emerged with a master's degree in English. His grandmother wanted him to go on for the Ph.D. degree then, but Turner made the decision to terminate his studies: "From a fairly early age, I was exercising an independence. I knew that decisions were going to be my own."

At that time Turner's decision was to get married and to get a job. He took a job on the faculty of Clark College in Atlanta, Georgia, the school at which his paternal grandfather had taught years before. After two years of college teaching, Turner now had family responsibilities, including a wife and a child. Because he had no job for the summer, he decided to go to Chicago, get a job with his father's assistance, and take a course in creative writing as a special student at the University of Chicago. He applied as a special student because, since the University of Cincinnati had rejected him as too young for doctoral study, he assumed that the University of Chicago would do the same. At registration time, however, Napier Wilt, who would be his advisor, informed him that he had been accepted as a regular student and encouraged him to take courses in the doctoral program in English. In the fall Turner moved his family to Chicago.

Turner then discovered that he could work forty hours a week (ten in his father's drugstore and thirty at the Quadrangle Club as a waiter) and study for the Ph.D. at the University of Chicago. Although working and studying, Turner earned as much money in Chicago as he had made working full time at Clark College. He did this and completed requirements for the doctoral degree in one academic year and three or four summers of residence. The degree was awarded in 1956, when Turner was twenty-five years old. Turner interrupted his doctoral work after one full year of studying to accept a faculty position at Morgan State College, a predominantly black school in Maryland.

CAREER

Stage I

As mentioned earlier, Turner's career began in 1949, when he was eighteen years old, seven years before he obtained the Ph.D. degree but immediately after the M.A. degree was awarded. That year, three major events occurred in Turner's life. He obtained a graduate degree, he married, and he took his first full-time job. This is how Turner launched stage I in his career.

The first stage extended over an eight-year period and included employment at two predominantly black schools in the South—Clark College in Atlanta, Georgia, and Morgan State College (later renamed Morgan State University) in Baltimore, Maryland. This stage in career development was interrupted by a year and three or four summers of graduate study.

Turner had a heavy teaching schedule and was engaged in extensive research for his dissertation, a study of American non-representational drama between 1920 and 1930. His creative output during this period involved quite a bit of poetry, a little fiction, and two television scripts; few of these creative works were published, perhaps only one short story. Turner said that he wrote his dissertation while teaching four English composition courses and one course in literature. Turner recalls that the president of Morgan State emphasized two things for his faculty—obtaining the doctorate and publishing. The emphasis on publishing was an encouragement to Turner, although he was unable to fulfill this interest during stage I. Turner remained at Morgan State five years, rising from instructor to assistant professor.

Stage II

After receiving his Ph.D. degree, Turner was offered a job at Florida A & M University, a predominantly black state-supported institution. He was appointed professor and chairman of the Department of English. His move to Florida began stage II in his career, which extended over a period of eleven years.

During this stage Turner made up for the publishing deficits of the first stage. Between the ages of twenty-six and thirty-eight, his career as a scholar began to bloom. He wrote two books—a volume of poetry in 1964 and the other, a study of Hawthorne's *Scarlet Letter* in 1967. His coedited book, *Images of the Negro in America*, was published by D. C. Heath in 1965. To this day, he describes the work on that book and its publication as "a very exciting experience" and often characterizes it as really "his first book." He also completed articles on several black writers for *Encyclopedia International* and *Encyclopedia Britannica*. From 1965 on, hardly a year passed that Turner was not asked to review a book for a scholarly publication such as the *College Language Association Journal* or *The Journal of Negro History*. His 1965 book launched him as a serious scholar recognized by his peers. Toward the end of the 1960s his career was coming into full bloom, after a slow start in stage I and the early years of stage II. Because of his administrative duties as department chairman, Turner said that he pushed his scholarly career ahead: "I always had the idea that the head of a department ought to publish too as a way of giving academic leadership to his faculty." Turner definitely provided such leadership during the years that he served as head of the English department, Agricultural and Technical State University in Greensboro.

Turner described the force that kept his scholarship alive as "strictly internal." He was not caught up in the well-known publish-or-perish syndrome. Even serving as a dean at the North Carolina Agricultural and Technical State University from 1966 to 1970—his third academic appointment to a predominantly black school—Turner described his position as a 9-to-5 job. "Then I would come home," he said, "and work on scholarship." He identified his publishing goal as that of educating a larger public than he could educate in a class. Clearly, writing had become a mission for him, a mission "to explain new ideas, introduce new authors." Again attempting to deny his deep respect for the contributions of humanists like himself, Turner attributed his writing in part to vanity. Such offhand attribution, however, is inconsistent with the seriousness with which Turner approaches his tasks. Sprinkled throughout his writings are the words *honesty* and *objectivity*. These words characterize the man and his work. Perhaps Turner is one who has been successful in the apprehension of others but less successful in perceiving himself—not an uncommon characteristic in scholars.

Darwin Turner has provided leadership as a scholar in a range of areas. His published works during the second stage of his career included original poems and analyses of fiction and drama that were created by both black and white scholars.

Indeed, Turner's earlier research was about American drama and Shakespeare. He studied both black and white artists and researched American and non-American writers because, in his words, "I didn't want to be one locked into the category of writing only about black subjects." His volume on Hawthorne; his review of Edna Ferber's *Ice Palace*; and his articles on the British playwrights Shakespeare, Osborne, and Auden attest to the range of his interests during stage II in his career.

Stage III

The third stage in Turner's career came soon after his second marriage, to Jean Turner, whom he describes as a "thoughtful" and "encouraging" person, (Turner 1971a, p.xiv), one who has the capacity to endure. Professionally an elementary school teacher, she both "revived" and "sustained" him at critical stages of his research and writing.

Coterminus with his new marriage, the spiral in his career that moved him toward increasing administrative responsibility from department chairman to dean of a graduate school seemed to have broken. With that break, stage III in his career began. The first three years were devoted wholly to scholarship—teaching, research, and writing. Turner actually planned to teach for approximately five years in a large university and then retuned to administration. As he put it, however, "Circumstances have worked otherwise." For the first time in a decade Turner was able to focus his concerns and to refine his skills in research and writing, although he feels at times that he did more while he was department head and dean than he has since. Although his current appointment at the University of Iowa involves some administrative duties, Turner feels that he was selected because of his research and writing.

Though not wishing to be limited to black literature, Turner stated that he enjoys it. Since his reputation is based in part on the work he has done in this field, he feels a responsibility to teach courses in black literature. Nevertheless, he continues to remind himself and others that his field is literature, "not just black literature." Therefore, one of four courses that he teaches each year is a nonblack course in the English department—for example, a drama course.

At this stage in Turner's career, his publications tend to emphasize the black experience because there is a need for more complete and objective studies of the works of black writers (Turner 1971a, p xxii), because "black writers . . . [are] in the vanguard of an artistic revolt" (Turner 1970, p. 163), and because he is "requested to prepare more materials for publication now" on the black experience.

Turner's personal and professional interest in black literature predates the current surge in public interests that began as the 1970s opened. His M.A. thesis, written in 1949, was on black writers. He presented the works of black writers in his courses at Clark, Florida A and M, and North Carolina A and T. Moreover, he presented papers on black writers at some professional association meetings during stages I and II of his career.

Thus Turner's focus on black writers during stage III of his career is due not so much to his own new special interest as to a new understanding in society at large. As Turner said, "From 1968 or 1969 to 1978 or so professional societies and publishers cried for something in black literature. Therefore, what went unpublished before, got published." For example, Turner said: "In 1965, I offered to deliver a paper on Jean Toomer to the South Atlantic Modern Language Association but was turned down. In 1969, the same group asked me to present whatever I wanted about black literature. In the 1970s the invitations to do things in black literature came so often that everything else was obscured."

Regarding the invitation to prepare materials for publication, Turner said that he experienced a dramatic increase when he moved from southern settings in predominantly black schools to predominantly white schools in the North. He noted that publishers' representatives come around the latter campuses and ask teachers what they are writing, but "publishers do not ask black scholars at black schools to prepare books. They look upon them as consumers of books." Turner, of course, views this practice as a form of discrimination. Of himself, he said, "I am no brighter than I was at the black schools." Nevertheless, as he moved North in 1969 to continue his career at the University of Wisconsin, the University of Michigan, and the University of Iowa and to begin stage III of his career, he received more and more invitations from more and more publishers to write.

In a single year, 1969, Turner published three edited volumes on *Black American Literature* with Charles Merrill and Company in Columbus, Ohio. One included essays; another, fiction; the third poetry. With sections on drama added, these volumes were reissued as a single book the following year. In 1971 Turner published an anthology of black drama (Turner, 1971b) and a book about three Afro-American writers and their search for identity (1971a). Two books followed in 1972—*Voices from the Black Experience: African* and *Afro-American Literature* (1972a), and *The Teaching of Literature by Afro-American Writers* (1972b). Some of these works were completed while Turner was in North Carolina, where his reputation began to grow during stage II.

Between 1969 and 1972, the first few years of stage III, Turner's creativity exploded. Freed of administrative responsibilities and encouraged by a new marriage, for a while he experienced unbridled creativity. Not only did he edit or write an average of two books every year as the 1970s began, but he also prepared chapters on black authors, black colleges, and Black Studies programs for approximately eight books; and wrote introductions to eight others (four books by black authors reissued by Arno Press and also books by or about blacks published by Collier, Merrill, Harper, and Lorrimer). Also during this period he reviewed five books by or about blacks for popular and professional magazines and published nine articles in scholarly journals.

The early years of the third stage in Turner's career as he approached and passed his fortieth birthday were brilliant, spectacular, extraordinary. For his unusual quantity of high-quality contributions, Turner was duly recognized first by the College Language Association, which gave him its 1971 Creative Scholarship Award, and then by the University of Chicago Alumni Association, which presented him with its Professional Achievement Award in 1972. Years later, in 1982, Turner was honored by the University of Cincinnati, which gave him a Distinguished Alumnus award and in

1983 he received an honorary doctorate from the University of Cincinnati.

Since the first burst during the early years of stage III, Turner's creative contributions have continued at a steady pace. Between 1973 and 1981 he averaged about one book every three years, a chapter in a book every year, and an article in a scholarly journal also annually.

During the 1970s, Turner was summoned into public affairs as a volunteer and asked to serve numerous public-service and professional associations. For example, he is on the board of trustees of the National Humanities Center. He has been on fellowship selection committees for the National Endowment for the Humanities (NEH), the American Council of Learned Societies, and the Rockefeller Foundation. For five years he directed an NEH-sponsored institute for improving research and teaching in Afro-American Studies. For the Modern Language Association he has served as a member of the board of directors and chairman of its Ethnic Studies Division. Likewise, he has served the National Council of Teachers of English as a director. Locally, he was the Iowa state chairman for a World Festival of Black and African Arts and Culture in the mid-1970s. Internationally, he was chosen as a U.S. delegate to the African Regional American Studies Conference, Ivory Coast, in 1976, and also to the World Festival of Black and African Arts and Culture, Nigeria, in 1977. Turner was invited to deliver a paper at the annual meeting of the teachers of foreign languages in Germany in 1982, and he addressed the English-language teachers of that country's national language association. These activities go far beyond Turner's duties as professor of English and chairman of an Afro-American Studies program, the dual positions Turner has occupied at the University of Iowa since 1972. The multiple requests for Turner's services at local, national, and international levels are indicative of his talent and the esteem of his peers.

Turner has been in the third stage of his career for about twelve years. He is at the midcentury mark in his life, a period when one usually shifts into stage IV of career development. It is not easy to predict the life process of an individual. To the extent that the past is prologue for the future, stage III in Turner's career has provided a fine foundation for stage IV. The uncoordinated themes of earlier years seem finally to have come together and consolidated into a harmonious whole.

REPUTATION AMONG PEERS

Darwin Turner and two other black scholars were nominated by leaders in the field as outstanding. A list of these three scholars was submitted to a representative national sample of black and of white professionals in English. The sample was obtained from the membership rosters of the College Language Association and the Modern Language Association. Of the 100 individuals who ranked the three nominees, 72 percent indicated that Turner was the most outstanding black scholar in English. Turner has received extensive recognition only within the past ten years; but his reputation has been maintained by a sustained output of high-quality works, which have been well received by his peers.

PERSONAL CHARACTERISTICS

Turner is a person for whom roots are important. He is proud of his family background. On a wall in their livingroom the Turners have an exhibit that consists of old photographs of both spouses' families and of their own three children. As mentioned earlier, Jeanne Turner has compiled scrapbooks of news stories, photographs, and Turner's certificates and awards of early achievement.

Turner obviously had the capacity to do good work, but he did not achieve his potential for scholarly achievement until the third stage in his career. Turner's tendency to compartmentalize his professional life and to rationalize the various compartments as complementary rather than contradictory may have interfered with his early development as a scholar. For example, at one point in his career he believed that "the jobs of administrator and teacher complement each other." Now that he has been freed from excessive administrative burdens and has experienced a burst of creative scholarship, he describes even "professional commitments, fellowship-selection committees, and other duties" as getting in the way of scholarship.

In college Turner had teachers whose instructional methods served as models. None, however, did he claim as mentors. Turner was an early achiever without a cheering squad, except perhaps his family. He was noticed but not nurtured by many of the adults in his life, but he claims that this was his own fault rather than theirs.

Turner has extremely high standards for himself and sometimes broods over whether he has done his best. With reference to writing, he said, "I always wanted to do the best kind of job I could. Although I am glad to be published, I usually am a little despondent because I know it is not exactly what I want." He said that his adult daughter has commented that he seldom gets excited over what he has done.

Turner has a profound commitment both to scholarship and to the humanities. He is critical of blacks and of others who "still believe that intelligent children should be directed only into fields where money is readily available such as medicine and law." He has found that "there is not the same kind of respect for a humanist, for an education that might bring internal reward but not financial reward." He is not sure that he sees "a major breakthrough" yet— "an increased respect among blacks or whites for work in the humanities."

Turner is disturbed about the absence of commitment to scholarship and to the humanities in our society generally. Personally, however, he has never been "very satisfied" and hence never fully committed to any of his professional positions, in the humanities or elsewhere. He stated that his feeling is not a reflection on the schools or the jobs but rather, represents his personal orientation. He believes that being "very satisfied" is a "stage [that] begins stagnation." Notwithstanding this feeling, Turner has been a faculty member at the University of Iowa for a decade, during which time his career has flourished. If he has not had complete satisfaction with his professional situation and personal circumstances, this has not been detrimental to his scholarly contribution. Although Turner may not want to let himself become fully committed to what he is doing, others are very satisfied with his output.

Turner is an able, honest, and competent scholar who renders objective appraisals. He is meticulous and careful, understanding and fair. He writes with courage and confidence, revealing both virtue and vice.

ANALYTIC SUMMARY

Acknowledging the interdependence between blacks and the society in which they live, Roger Rosenblatt said that American literary conventions have provided black writers both something to lean on and something to push against. Darwin Turner made a similar observation when he said of black essayists that they came of age, then rejected the age. This experience of becoming a part of and separating oneself from is continuous and is found in every system in society. It is a process that is particularly agonizing in the kinship system.

Turner was part of a family of orientation in which the attainment of higher education was a tradition. This orientation supported his early academic achievements. Yet he felt compelled to separate himself from moving in lockstep from one level of educational achievement to the next as quickly as he could. He rejected his family's advice to study for a doctoral degree immediately after completing his master's degree. Instead, he married, began his career, and became a father.

Turner moved directly from a family of orientation that succored and supported him through the first level of graduate study into a family of procreation. He skipped the transitional stage of independent householder and the opportunity this status provides to observe and consider new strategies for living. Because he arrived at his new family status before he turned twenty-one years old, Turner had to give succor and support to others despite his continuing need for nurturing. The burden was overwhelming and took its toll, eventually resulting in divorce.

When a career is launched before formal education is complete, there may be indecision regarding vocation. This certainly was Turner's experience. Turner resisted committing his future to education even after he became a candidate for the doctoral degree. The interruption with marriage and work of Turner's progression through graduate education complicated the early stage of his career development as a scholar. Because of the requirements of supervised and approved graduate study and the household responsibilites of a new family unit, little time was available for research and writing.

Although Turner's doctorate was awarded when he was only twenty-five years old, by the time he had achieved it his career was in progress, with six years of employment behind him. He was ready, he believed, to take on academic administration as a department chairman and eventually as a dean. The pressures of administration are persistent, however; Turner could continue a developed career in scholarship and link it with new responsibilities in administation only by limiting the time devoted to each. Thus, it is more difficult to start a career in scholarship while serving as an administrator at the same time. Turner tried to do this, but he could do it only at the price of compartmentalizing his life—walling off one side of his career from the other, practicing administration by day and scholarship at night. Such a strategy leaves little time for family socialization.

Though fragile and vulnerable, the kinship system is significant—both the family of orientation and that of procreation—it can orient a person toward or away from education. It can enhance or retard the development of a career. Turner's career clearly accelerated as he moved into its third stage. He was energized and sustained by the nurturance of a new marriage effected when he was more mature—when the doubt of vocation had been resolved, the burden of graduate education was behind him, and the publicity surrounding his preprofessional early achievement had faded. This second marriage has endured thirteen years to the date of this interview.

In light of Turner's life history, one may hypothesize that there is an association between education and career development and that the completion of graduate education helps launch an academic career but that earlier education has little effect unless it is capped by a doctoral degree. Further, one may hypothesize that an association exists between the kinship system and education and that the family may orient one toward education and facilitate its acquisition as long as one remains in its care; the family of procreation may retard the tempo with which one obtains a graduate education if it is formed while one is in midcourse.

Finally, in light of this life history, one may hypothesize that early acceleration in one's education does not guarantee an outstanding beginning for one's career, but that an unexceptional career beginning does not preclude either spectacular growth along the way or perhaps, a fruitful conclusion to one's career.

CHAPTER 7

The Stages of a Scholar's Life: Career, Education, and Family

THE GOAL OF THIS STUDY was to discover the stages of development of outstanding black scholars and to assess the factors that led to their achievements.

In education, William Boyd found that blacks in predominantly white colleges are often insulted by the inference that they are "special admission" students. "The main stereotype," he reported, "is that blacks are so different and deficient that increased equal opportunity in higher education can occur only if colleges lower their academic standards"(Boyd 1974, p. 4). This study will shed light on the truth or falsity of this and several other racial stereotypes. Five black scholars who were praised by their professional colleagues in the social sciences and the humanities were discovered. They are John Hope Franklin, W. Arthur Lewis, Kenneth B. Clark, Matthew Holden, Jr., and Darwin T. Turner. What were the life processes and the events that developed our five candidates into the scholars that they are?

Manfred Stanley states that *organism* is one of two master metaphors of Western civilization; the other is *mechanism* (Stanley 1978, p.137). These two have been used often to organize data for scientific analysis. Floyd Allport describes social organisms as self-limiting, unified, dynamic structures or systems that are ongoing through events that both link and separate the processes and relate that which is inside the system to that which is outside (Allport 1955, pp. 615–619). As stated earlier, the event-structure theoretical framework of Floyd Allport is used to help discover critical events in the life histories of the scholars. Stages in their career-development process and the presence, if any, of consistent patterns among the five scholars will be identified. The ideal-type construction resulting from this analysis of the consolidated careers of the five scholars may be applicable to others in the social sciences and the humanities. Further research, of course, will be necessary to verify this claim.

That these findings regarding the stages in a scholar's life are derived from racial minorities does not necessarily mean that they are not representative of other population groups. Robert Merton stated that "not infrequently . . . the . . . minority in a society represents the interests and ultimate values of the group more effectively than the . . . majority" (Merton 1968, p. 421).

In some respects this study is in the tradition of Daniel J. Levinson's research and is a further test of his theories presented in *The Seasons of a Man's Life* (Levinson 1978). Departing from the model of Erikson, who regards development as a series of stages in ego development, our analysis is closer to the concept of *life structure* formulated by Levinson and his collaborators. This concept "is centered more directly on the boundary between self and the world. It gives equal consideration to self and world as aspects of the lived life" (Levinson 1978, p. 323).

FREEDOM, AN EXTERNAL POSSIBILITY

The approach of this study differs from that of Levinson in that it considers career development as a sequence of structured events or a system interacting with, but conceptually different from, both the family or kinship system and the education system. Whereas Levinson consolidates these, analyzing the sequence of periods in development, this study disaggregates the systems and analyzes career, family, and education separately and only then as one consolidated system. The difference mentioned, however, is more stylistic than substantive, having to do largely with technique of analysis.

If there is a fundamental difference between the approach of this study and that of Levinson, it has to do with the assumptions. We do not assume that the various periods in adult development are in "a fixed sequence," that the various periods must be "traversed . . . in the order given ," and that one cannot skip a period (Levinson 1978, p. 319). The concept of life-structure development in stages is accepted as a useful metaphor that aids in ordering the analysis of the career of scholars; but the metaphor should not be reified. Indeed, the concept of stage development was almost rejected as a redaction because of the initial difficulty it created for the analysis.

Freedom is an eternal possibility in human social relations. Choice and purpose are of the essence. Although habit and custom often becloud these facts and make them difficult to comprehend, they exist nevertheless, whether or not one acknowledges choice and purpose in human circumstances. Thus an analytic concept that violated these basic assumptions would be of limited value in explaining social aspects of the human enterprise such as career, education, and family development. In effect, Levinson acknowledges this assumption about freedom when he said, "the developmental periods are age-linked but they are not a simple derivative of age" (Levinson 1978, p. 319).

STAGED DEVELOPMENT AND CHOICE

The concept of stage development was of value, however, because the stages tend to be sequential and appear to be fixed. Thus Levinson's description of how the sequence works can be embraced because of this tendency and appearance:

> During the current period, a man works chiefly on the developmental tasks of this period. But he also does some work on the tasks of other periods. Tasks that will become primary in later periods may be activated early. The tasks of preceding periods are not completed and cast aside when those periods come to an end. If they are worked out reasonably well at the appropriate time, they continue to support further development in subsequent periods. Gains of the past form the ground on which current developmental efforts are built [Levinson 1978, p. 321].

If this statement is accepted as an appropriate description of the developmental process, one recognizes that people go through a series of tasks that appear to be beyond choice or control, not so much because they are as because the tasks are shared in common with others and therefore cannot be easily changed unilaterally. One is not fully in control of what happens in the unfolding of a career through numerous stages. One may affirm oneself; but confirmation must originate with others. Most of us in human society eventually learn that our affirmed self-interest is accommodated favorably and confirmed by others only if we respond from time to time in ways that confirm and fulfill their self-interest. Reciprocity and mutuality indicate that none is fully in control of his or her fate.

Although one moves inexorably through the stages of development from one level to another, one tends to do this because of habit on the one hand and custom on the other, and not because the stages are fixed or movement is inflexible. They merely *appear* to be fixed and inflexible.

A concept of stage development that acknowledges choice and purpose in human social relations accepts the possibility that the sequence of development may change, including skipping ahead and falling behind. Because deviations from the conventional involve mutual decisions by the initiator of action and those who must respond, and because the initiator of action can never completely control the responses of others, deviations from agreed-upon means usually are implemented at the risk of disapproval of one party to the interaction process because of discomfort as a result of disruption of customary ways of doing things. Most people, not wishing to experience disapproval, behave in customary ways.

The goal of this study was to discover customary ways in which successful scholars in U.S. society have developed. Specifically, we wanted to know how outstanding black scholars achieved eminence in a society where they are members of a minority population. During the course of this study, Levinson's statement that "we need great wisdom lest we evaluate too superficially" (1978, p. 320) was a constant warning against premature conclusions.

Case studies of the life histories of each of the five scholars were analyzed to discover clues to their development. Information was obtained from analysis of personal interviews; curricula vitae; biographical sketches in *Who's Who in America, American Men and Women of Science, Social Science Citation Index,* and *Who's Who in Black America;* and books and articles written by the scholars.

Because our goal is to develop an ideal-type model of stage development for black intellectuals, only averages for the five scholars are reported in Tables 7–1, 7–2, and 7–3. However, the variations of individuals around averages will be discussed. For each scholar, the age at the beginning of a stage, critical events that contributed to the end or beginning of a stage, and the length of each stage in the scholar's career are analyzed separately and then together.

CAREER STAGES

The five scholars in the humanities and the social sciences have careers that separate into four stages. Stage I begins around twenty-four years of age and usually consists of such scholarly activity as teaching, research, and writing. It lasts six to seven years. Stage II begins around thirty or thirty-one years of age and lasts eight to nine years. It consists largely of teaching, research, writing, and public service. Stage III is a period for refining the teaching, research, and writing skills developed in the first two stages; expanding one's

Table 7-1

Stages in a Scholar's Career (Combined Experiences of Franklin, Lewis, Clark, Holden, Turner), 1981

Characteristics of Career	Average Age, Year, and Number
Stage I Teaching, research, writing	
Beginning age	23.8
Length in years	6.6
Stage II Teaching, research, writing, public service	
Beginning age	30.4
Length in years	8.8
Stage III Teaching, research, writing, public service, administration	
Beginning age	39.2
Length in years	11.4
Stage IV Teaching, research, writing, public service, administration, leadership of learned societies	
Beginning age	51
Length in years in progress	15.3
Other career characteristics	
Number of years in education	32.8
Number of years in administration	10.4
Number of different colleges of employment	4
Years of longest service to a single school	18.4
Number of articles published	52.5
Number of books written or edited	11.6
Age at publication of first article	26.6
Age at publication of first book	32.6
Age at publication of most recent article	58.6
Age at publication of most recent book	55.2
Years between publication of first and most recent article	32
Years between publication of first and most recent book	23.6
Age of presidency of leading U.S. professional association	60

participation in public affairs; and possibly developing administrative skills. This stage begins around the age of thirty-nine and extends over a period of ten to eleven years. Stage IV begins at the midcentury point in a scholar's life, around the fifty-first year. In this stage all skills developed during the previous periods are consolidated into a complementary pattern, and administrative skills may be further developed. Responsibility for the leadership of learned societies is assumed during this period. Stage IV may last from fifteen to nineteen years, depending on age of retirement.

In summary, each stage refines the skills developed in previous stages and initiates new skills. Moreover, the length of time that one spends in a stage gradually increases as one passes through higher stages: six to seven years in the first, eight to nine in the second,

Table 7-2
Educational Stages in a Scholar's Life (Combined Experiences of
Franklin, Lewis, Clark, Holden, Turner), 1981

Educational Characteristics	Average Age, Year, and Number
Stages I and II Preschool, Elementary, and Secondary School	
Ending age	15
Length in years	15
Stage III College	
Ending age	20
Length in years	5
Stage IV Graduate Education	
Ending age	26.4
Length in years (from bachelor's to doctor's)	6.4
Length in years (from bachelor's to master's)	1.8
Length in years (from master's to doctor's)	5.5
Relationship between education and career	
Age at beginning of stage I in career	23.8
Length in years (from end of college to beginning of career)	3.8
Length in years (career began *before* Ph.D. study ended)	3.8
Length in years (career began *after* Ph.D. study ended)	2
Relationship between education and family	
Age at marriage	26.2
Length in years (from end of college to beginning of marriage)	6.5
Length in years (marriage began *before* Ph.D. study ended)	3.3
Length in years (marriage began *after* Ph.D. study ended)	4.5

eleven to twelve in the third, and fifteen to nineteen in the fourth. As one works out one's career from stage to succeeding stage, one assumes new responsibilities in each new stage and therefore has more time than one had in the previous stage to assimilate new responsibility with previous obligations.

Levinson's statement about the absence of variability in age around the beginning and ending of a stage is in part confirmed and in part contradicted by this analysis (Levinson 1978, p. 318). In each of the four stages, a majority of the five scholars are within one to four years of the age of the other scholars at the beginning of a period. This is a relatively narrow range of variability. Yet the total variability by age is as great as ten years for all five scholars in stages I and II, and as much as eight years in stages III and IV. When one considers that the lengths of stages I and II are six to seven years, and eight to nine years, respectively, a variability of ten years is great.

Often one and usually not more than two scholars account for the wide variability. For example, in stage I four of the scholars were

Table 7-3

Family Stages in a Scholar's Life (Combined Experiences of Franklin, Lewis, Clark, Holden, Turner), 1981

Family Characteristics	Average Age, Year, and Number
Stage I Family of orientation (offspring receiving)	
Ending age	21.2
Length in years	21.2
Stage II Independent householder (offspring in own home)	
Ending age	28.3
Length in years	6.3
Stage III Family of procreation (parent giving)	
Length of years (in progress)	33.4
Other family characteristics	
Age at initial marriage	26.2
Number of marriages	1.2
Number of children in household	2.2
Relationship between the family and career	
Age at beginning of career	23.8
Length in years (of marriage before career began)	4
Length in years (of marriage after career began)	4

within a five-year age range, but one deviated from the top of the five-year range by ten years. Stage IV had been reached by only three of the five scholars. Only a one-year difference separated the ages at which two of the scholars reached this stage. One scholar, however, was seven years above the age of the youngest scholar when he reached stage IV.

Not only did one and sometimes two scholars deviate widely from the norm with reference to age of entry into a stage, but at least one of the five took twice as long to finish a stage as did the scholar who most rapidly passed through the stage. Because of this finding, one questions the rigid age pattern that some would impose on the stages of adult development. Although most individuals enter and complete a stage within a customary interval, one person here and there will not conform to that pattern.

It is the person who violates the norm who should interest social scientists. He or she tells us a lot about the flexibility of the human condition. We want to know whether a person who lags behind, remains behind. Likewise, does a person who lurches ahead stay ahead? The answer to both questions is negative. Some scholars spend too little time maturing in one stage and have to make up what they missed in the next, in addition to doing the regular tasks of that stage. Other scholars prematurely take on responsibilities in one stage that are more appropriate for the next stage. Thus the lower stage may be prolonged so that the usual tasks of that stage can be performed along with the added responsibilities.

Tasks in stages I and II are commonly traded back and forth by scholars. Of our five scholars, two waited until as late as stage III, which normally occurs between forty and fifty years of age, to make up for scholarly activities that should have been performed earlier. Stage III is about the last opportunity one has to make up deficiencies if one wishes to bring ·one's career to a successful conclusion as an outstanding scholar during the fifteen to nineteen years of stage IV. The two scholars who waited until stage III to catch up were extraordinarily productive of scholarly works between forty and fifty years of age. They caught up, demonstrating that the adult life structure is flexible and responsive to compensatory action. However, the individual pays a price when professional activity that should have been spread over several years is concentrated into a shorter period. Thus the stages for scholarly development and their age ranges are normative by prevailing custom. Individuals may tailor their adaptation to the various stages, but with consequences if the adaptations vary from custom. Nevertheless, variations are possible.

As a final point regarding variability in age at which one enters a career stage and length of time required to complete it, this analysis reveals that one who enters a stage at the youngest age does not necessarily complete the stage in the shortest period of time. Also, one who is the oldest upon entering a stage does not necessarily remain in that stage longer than others. Levinson is correct in his statement that "the life cycle is an organic whole" and that "the past and future are in the present" (Levinson 1978, p. 321). The past, present, and future condition each other; but human experience usually provides for compensatory action. As long as choice and purpose exist, the present is never fixed. Rather, it can be modified to accommodate the past and to anticipate the future. Such a modification in light of the past and the future can occur at any developmental stage. In social and psychological systems, nothing is forever fixed and unchangeable.

OTHER RESEARCH

Our findings regarding compensatory action as a fundamental part of the social system, including the career-development process of scholars in the humanities and the social sciences, is corroborated by other research such as the studies on creativity by Harvey Lehman (Lehman 1946, 460–480;1947, pp. 342–356), and the study of early-maturing and late-maturing boys by Mary Cover Jones (Jones 1960; 804–822).

Lehman reported that "the renowned benefactors of humanity
. . . were less than twenty-five years old at the time they did their most
creative work." His statement applied to 56 percent of the chemists,
53 percent of the mathematicians, 53 percent of distinguished
authors, and 30 percent of eminent philosophers (1946, pp. 478–
479). This finding also means that more than 40 percent of the
scientists and humanists made renowned contributions to their fields
after the age of twenty-five. The reciprocal figure is often forgotten,
however. For example, Lehman found that about 12 percent of
psychologists, 8 percent of economists and political scientists, and 4
percent of writers published creative works after the age of sixty
(Lehman 1946, p. 355). This is further evidence that catch-up time is
possible in some fields. It may be experienced by only a few; but these
few exceptions prove the rule that the stages of adult development are
not rigid, fixed, and unaccommodating to varying temporal patterns
of individual adaptation.

Lehman discovered one individual in his studies of creative
output who made his "first and notable chemistry contribution as
late as age 75." On the basis of this finding, Lehman said, "it seems
logical to infer that, although there is no deadline beyond which it is
impossible to make one's initial contribution, age 75 is too old to
start contributing if one hopes to make more than one important
contribution" (Lehman 1946, p. 466). This, essentially, is one of the
consequences or prices of delaying and deferring tasks to a later stage
that should be dealt with in an earlier one: One's total scholarly
output is likely to be reduced (Lehman 1946, p. 470).

Further evidence that catch-up time is possible is provided by
Jones's study of the adult careers of early-maturing and late-
maturing boys. Jones said that it is well known that "early- or late-
maturing may have a considerable bearing upon the social life and
personal adjustment of some individuals during . . . adolescence."
But what of the long-term effects? Jones found that the early-
maturing teenagers showed marked differences in size, strength, and
attractiveness of physique. The early-maturing boys also were judged
to be more relaxed than were the late-maturing adolescents. She
found, however, that by the age of thirty-three differences in size of
the two groups had diminished to insignificance. Each group showed
considerable overlap in manifestation of masculine characteristics;
the two groups also were similar in socioeconomic status and in level
of education obtained.

As stated before, there are consequences for starting ahead or
lagging behind. These consequences may be positive or negative.
One consequence for the late-maturing adolescents that manifested
itself during adulthood was a more flexible attitude. Jones speculates
that "in the course of having to adapt to difficult status problems, the
late-maturers gained some insights and are indeed more flexible
while the early-maturing, capitalizing on their ability to make a good

impression, may have clung to their earlier success pattern . . .
becoming somewhat rigid" (Jones 1960; pp. 812, 805–814).

Our finding that those who start out ahead do not always stay
ahead is corroborated by the findings not only of Jones but also of
Terman and Oden (1947, p. 194), who studied 781 individuals who
were among the top 1 percent of intelligent people in the United
States, according to standardized tests. The mean age at high school
graduation was at least a year below the average for others in their
state; moreover, of those respondents whose education had ended
before the follow-up study, 90 percent of the men and 86 percent of
the women entered college. Approximately 30 percent, however, did
not graduate from college. About 20 percent of the sample had not
begun to fulfill their potential, according to these researchers. Clearly
the ability was present, but other things interfered.

In addition to identifying the stages of scholarly development,
the ideal-type scholar's career contribution to the field of education
and to the literature of his discipline is analyzed. The analysis begins
with one's service in the field of education because it is the principal
institutional context for the career of most scholars in the humanities
and the social ssciences.

The average scholar in this study, as seen in Table 7–1 has been
in education about a third of a century, representing 90 percent of his
professional career. He has been affiliated with about four different
colleges or universities, for an average term of eight years at each
school. Actually, the pattern of service involves fewer years on the
faculty of the first schools of employment and more years at the most
recent schools of employment.

The longest service the scholars had rendered a single school
averaged eighteen years. This figure represented exceptional continuity; but it is heavily weighted by data for one scholar, whose
entire career was spent at one institution. Discounting the effect of his
experience, the average is still thirteen years, indicating a remarkable
amount of institutional loyalty.

There is debate about whether administration and scholarship
are compatible or incompatible activities. Scholars disagree on this
matter. It would appear, however, based on their experience, that
administration is a component of educational leadership in the
careers of those who are outstanding, and must be accommodated at
some stage in one's career, usually in stages III and IV. The scholars
in this study devoted ten to eleven years to administration as
departmental chairman, dean, or president of an educational
institution and as administrators in governmental or private con-
sulting agencies. This average is weighted by data for one scholar
who devoted twice as much time to administration as did any of the
others. When his experience is discounted, the administrative
commitment remains at about seven to eight years, approximately
one-quarter of the average time the scholars worked in the field of

education. Thus one may expect the ideal-type scholar to spend from one-quarter to one-third of his or her career in administration. This may come as a surprise to some, but it is probably what may be expected by those who lead the field.

The publishing experience of the scholars in this study is extensive. These men began publishing early in their career and published steadily over the years. As Lehman said, "our most distinguished creative thinkers have usually possessed, among other things, an astonishing capacity for hard patient work" (1946; p. 474). The productivity of our scholars represents such work. They have written or edited an average of eleven to twelve books, and published an average of fifty-two to fifty-three articles in learned journals. They began publishing at a relatively early age. Their first articles were published when they were twenty-six to twenty-seven years old only two to three years after the start of their professional career. An average of about six years after the first article appeared, some of the scholars produced a book. At this point in their career, they were an average of thirty-two to thirty-three years old, with eight to nine years on the job, and solidly in the second stage of career development. The life span of creativity of the five sholars in terms of number of years between first and current article averaged a quarter of a century.

The most creative work is not always completed at an early age. Lehman found this pattern: "the major contributors to a given field accomplished their first important research at younger average ages and their last important work at older average ages" (1946; p. 467). The younger starters, however, tend to exhibit greater productivity (Lehman, 1946; p. 474).

"On the whole . . . those destined to go far have started early and moved rapidly" (Lehman 1946; p. 479). Shakespeare and Dickens are examples of this principle. Their first contributions were published at the age of twenty-four and twenty-one,respectively. Shakespeare's publishing career extended over a range of twenty-five years and Dickens's over a range of thirty-six years (Lehman 1946; p. 471). These individuals were not unlike two scholars discussed herein— Franklin and Lewis. Franklin's first article was published when he was twenty-three years old and Lewis's first article when he was twenty-four. Both have continued to publish steadily for more than forty years.

In summary, the publishing pattern of the ideal-type scholar begins with a contribution of articles to learned journals early in the first stage of one's career, when one is twenty-six to twenty-seven years old, and then continues, maybe with a book, half a dozen years later after one has entered the second stage of one's career. Thereafter one probably will publish an article every two years and eventually write or edit about a dozen books during the course of a productive career that may extend over at least a quarter of a century.

EDUCATIONAL STAGES

As mentioned earlier, educational development is analyzed as a process both related to and separate from the structured events of a career. Four educational stages are identified—I and II; preschool and the primary and secondary grades; III; college; and IV, graduate education. In the analysis, the age at which a scholar enters and exits a stage was determined. Also, education and its relationship to career development and family structure was examined.

As seen in Table 7-2, all scholars in this study completed secondary school on time— probably ahead of time, in terms of the age at which they graduated. None was over 16 years old; two were even younger. These scholars completed stages I and II of their education with dispatch and moved immediately into college.

According to this analysis, the ideal-type scholar commences adulthood with college degree in hand. The average age at graduation for the ideal-type scholars is twenty. Scholars in this study fulfilled the requirements of college and stage III before they were called on to assume other adult responsibilities. Straightaway, they enrolled for the master's degree—all except one who matriculated immediately for the doctorate.

The scholars earned a Master of Arts of Master of Science degree in one to two years and graduated at the average age of twenty-one or twenty-two. The master's is the first-level degree of stage IV, graduate education; this stage ends when one has obtained a doctoral degree. All except one scholar immediately enrolled for a doctorate after receiving a master's degree. Thus there was continuity in their formal education. Five to six years later, the scholars had doctoral degrees. The ideal-type scholar completes formal education at the age of twenty-six or twenty-seven.

The ideal-type scholar moves immediately from one stage of educational development to the next. Within a stage, however, one may hop, skip, and jump, as most of the scholars did in elementary or secondary school in stage II, and as one of the scholars did in graduate school in stage IV.

Three scholars took time out before studying for the doctoral degree. This is the first respite that any of the scholars permitted himself during his educational odyssey. None let up before receiving the master's degree. After that, time out was called for not more than three years; in most instances, the time out was even less. This interlude was used largely to replenish depleted finances.

Probably more important than the young age of the scholars is the short period they required to obtain the Ph.D. degree. They were in, through, and out of graduate school before other concerns could distract them.

That the scholars in this study had limited finances is indicated by the fact that most had to begin their professional careers before receiving the doctoral degree, although they received it at an early age. To support themselves while finishing their studies, they signed on as teachers in colleges and universities—some part time and others full time. These jobs launched the careers of the scholars in education. This was the experience of most of the scholars who entered their profession when they were twenty-three to twenty-four years old, a few years before their doctorates were awarded. The scholars have remained members of the teaching profession, which they entered in early adulthood. All continued to be affiliated with an academy.

The need to work may have been an asset providing a precept-and-example experience of what the life of scholarship is about, a reinforcement of an earlier vocational choice. Thus the ideal-type scholar may serve more or less as an apprentice for three to four years before fully credentialed. When it comes too early, full-time work may interfere with fulfillment of student status; it both enhances the ending of formal education and helps the beginning of a professional career.

FAMILY STAGES

How is the kinship system related to the other two? The kinship system exists in three stages: I, the family of orientation, in which the offspring receives nurturance, support, protection, and unconditional love; II, the independent householder, an experimental period in transition without the responsibility and obligation of commitment to a significant other; and III, the family of procreation, in which the parent gives nurturance, support, protection, and unconditional love.

The roles and responsibilities in the kinship system are further evidence that stage development is neither rigid nor fixed. Indeed, the survival of the kinship system depends on choice and purpose, certainly not on inflexible qualities. Yet the family is often stereotyped in form and function. It, more than any other social system, is influenced by custom; this accounts for its highly regularized ways.

As seen in Table 7–3, the ideal-type scholar is nurtured, supported, and protected in a family of orientation from birth to the age of twenty-one or twenty-two. It would appear that two full decades of nurturance, support, and unconditional love are necessary to prepare one for a scholarly career of independent inquiry, conceptual analysis, and creative synthesis.

As mentioned before, compensatory action is an ever-present possibility in social and psychological activity. A two-person household is the conventional way of caring for offspring in a family. Scholars in this study, however, prospered in a number of alternative arrangements that functioned fully as families and that fulfilled all the family's responsibilities and commitment to the offspring. These scholars came of age in nuclear families, extended families, blended families, one-parent families. Whatever the household composition, adult members were nurturing, supportive, and loving. These ideal-type scholars are a reflection of such care.

More important than household composition is the temporal period of support that an offspring received. Premature withdrawal of support probably would have stunted the educational development of these scholars. A stunted education in turn could have interfered with professional opportunities in a chosen vocation. The premature withdrawal of support to offspring may have severe repercussions.

The scholars in this study received direct and full family support during preschool, primary, and secondary school years, and through college. They remained as official household members of the family of orientation while moving through these levels of educational development. Three scholars remained in the family of orientation until they obtained the master's degree. With this positive social and emotional family support, the scholars moved rapidly through their education without much interruption.

The transitional period is stage II, when one leaves the parental household. This ranged from two to ten years for four of our scholars. One scholar skipped this period altogether and immediately formed a family of procreation as he left the household of his family of orientation. An individual is free to change customary ways of doing things; but, as mentioned, there are consequences with which one must then live.

The scholars in this study did several things during the transitional stage. One had to earn sufficient funds and then go back to school. Another was involved in establishing himself in a new physical and spiritual environment. Still another had sufficient scholarship money if supplemented with menial work but no support for dissertation research. The transitional, independent-householder period lasted six to seven years for four of the scholars. None married before age twenty-four; two waited until their thirties.

The transitional stage gets its name from the kinship system, but it is also related to education and work. Before marriage, two scholars obtained a doctoral degree, four acquired a master's degree; all had the baccalaureate degree well in hand an average of six to seven years before marriage. Graduate study usually came during the period of transition in family status. It appears that marriage is postponed during the transitional years to accommodate higher education for the ideal-type scholar who aspires to achieve the highest academic degree.

At the end of the transitional period, three things happened suddenly. Three scholars received professional appointments while single and before they received the Ph.D. After working two to four years, all married. Only one scholar married before he received a permanent appointment.

In summary, the first priority of the scholars in this study was to obtain higher education, including graduate study. The second priority was to start a career; the third priority was marriage. None married before the bachelor's degree was received; all were still single when they received the master's degree. Three married before receiving the doctor's degree, and two married after receiving it. Most of these changes occurred during stage II, the age of transition that began at age twenty-one or twenty-two and extended to twenty-eight or twenty-nine. After that, stage III in the family took over.

Among our scholars, stage III has been a long-lasting experience. It is the period when the family of procreation nurtures and cares for its offspring while the scholar is developing a professional career. Formal study for education is over. Marriage and an outstanding career as a scholar seem to go hand in hand, as far as the ideal-type scholar is concerned. They appear to stabilize each other. The scholars in this study had magnificent careers; they married when they were twenty-six to twenty-seven years old, two to three years after their careers had begun. At the time of the interviews, they had been married an average of 33 years. They also had been outstanding and productive scholars. Their households consisted of an average of two children.

CONCLUSION

This analysis indicates that career, education, and family development processes are relatively independent in that each process has a life range of its own and a sequence of stages that are system-specific. The analysis also reveals that these structures or systems are interrelated–that events in one system condition happenings in another.

It was particularly interesting to analyze the convergence of events in all three systems during the transitional stage of independent householder in the kinship system. Within a short period of time, scholars started their professional careers, married, and ended their formal education. Not by chance did these happenings occur almost simultaneously in each of the three systems. One may conclude that these are covariant events, each influenced by happenings outside its own system.

As a source of power, the career system is unchallenged. It certainly was primary in the public identity of the five scholars and their households. Because of career achievements, the scholars received multiple honors.

A career as a scholar, however, is greatly assisted by formal education. Higher education at the graduate school level is necessary–although it may not be sufficient–for attaining the status of a scholar. The credentialing function of formal education gives it an authoritative position in our society. Education has less power to grant the privileges and prerogatives that a successful career in scholarship can convey, but its authority is overwhelming as a sanctioning agency for academic standards. Hence it is the midwife for most professional careers, including a career in scholarship. Education, then, is the second most powerful system in the life of a scholar.

Least powerful is the kinship system; yet this system is the most enduring. It is the structure through which young people receive nurturance, support, and protection; and through which adults provide that nurturance, support, and protection. The family system is fragile, and family members are vulnerable. They are sustained by unconditional love, which all may give but which any can withhold and none can be compelled to give. When love is withheld, such action threatens the stability of the family structure.

Despite its weak and vulnerable structure, the family remains essential in educational and career development. It can orient one toward or away from extended formal schooling. It can stabilize or disrupt a professional career. The family of orientation is concerned with the former; the family of procreation with the latter. None who would be an ideal-type scholar married until he had achieved a master's degree, obtained in most instances with full family support. The outstanding scholars in this study had decades of marriage behind them to spouses with whom there existed mutual respect and affection.

Without support of the family, educational and professional achievement is very difficult. Neither system is able to stand alone.

References

Allport, Floyd A. 1955. *Theories of Perception and the Concept of Structure.* New York: Wiley.

Barron's Educational Services (BES). *Profile of American Colleges.* Woodbury, N.Y.

Bowles, Samuel and Gintis, Herbert. 1976. *Schooling in Capitalist America.* New York: Basic Books.

Boyd, William M. II. 1974. *Desegregating America's Colleges.* New York: Praeger.

Brown vs. Board of Education. 1954. 347 U.S. 483.

Browning, Jane E. Smith, and Williams, John B. 1978. "History and Goals of Black Institutions of Higher Learning." In Charles V. Willie and Ronald B. Edmonds, eds, *Black Colleges in America.* New York: Teachers College Press, pp. 68–93.

Clark, Kenneth B. 1940. "Some Factors Influencing the Remembering of Prose Material." *Archives of Psychology* 253: 1–73.

_____. 1951. *Effect of Prejudice and Discrimination on Personality Development.* Washington, D.C.: Mid-Century White House Conference on Children.

_____. 1955. *Prejudice and Your Child.* Boston: Beacon Press.

_____.1965. *Dark Ghetto.* New York: Harper.

_____.1972. *A Possible Reality.* New York: Emerson Hall.

_____.1974. *Pathos of Power.* New York: Harper & Row.

_____. 1978. "Kenneth B. Clark." In Thomas C. Hunter, ed., *Beginnings.* New York: Crowell, pp. 76–84.

Clark, Kenneth B. and Clark, Mamie P. 1947. "Racial Identification and Preference in Negro Children." In Theodore M. Newcomb and Eugene Hartley, eds., *Readings in Social Psychology.* New York: Holt, pp. 169–178.

Coleman, Richard P., and Rainwater, Lee. 1978. *Social Standing in America.* New York: Basic Books.

DuBois, W. E. B. 1903. *The Souls of Black Folk.* Chicago: Clury.

Duncan, Beverly, and Duncan, Otis. 1970. "Family Stability and Occupational Success." In Charles V. Willie, ed., *The Family Life of Black People*. Columbus, Ohio: Merrill, pp. 156–177.

Elam, J. Corene. 1981. Review of *The Wayward and the Seeking* (Darwin T. Turner, ed.), *Journal of Negro History* 66 (Spring): 55–56.

Evans, Richard I. 1980. *The Making of Social Psychology*. New York: Gardner Press.

Franklin, John Hope. 1938. "Edward Bellamy and the Naturalist Movement." *New England Quarterly* (December).

_____. 1956. *The Militant South*. Cambridge, Mass.: Harvard University Press.

_____. 1960. "As for Our History." In Charles Griersellers, Jr., ed., *The Southerner as American*. Chapel Hill: University of North Carolina Press, pp. 3–18.

_____. 1974. *From Slavery to Freedom*, 4th ed. New York: Knopf. 4th ed. Originally 1947.

_____. Starr, Isidore, 1967. *The Negro in Twentieth Century.*. New York: Vintage Books.

Franklin, John Hope, 1976. *Southern Odyssey*. Baton Rouge: Louisiana State University Press.

Freeman, Richard B. 1976a. *The Over-Educated American*. New York: Academic Press.

_____. 1976b. *Black Elite*. New York: McGraw-Hill.

Goode, William J. 1973. *Explorations in Social Theory*. New York: Oxford University Press.

Gurin, Patricia, and Epps, Edgar. 1975. *Black Consciousness, Identity and Achievement*. New York: Wiley.

Hauser, Robert, and Featherman, David. 1977. *The Process of Stratification*. New York: Academic Press.

Hawley, Willis D. 1981. "Increasing the Effectiveness of School Desegregation: Lessons from Research." In Adam Yarmolinsky *et al.* eds., *Race and Schooling in the City*. Cambridge, Mass.: Harvard University Press, pp. 145–162.

Health Resources Administration. 1977. *An Exploratory Evaluation of U.S. Medical Schools' Efforts to Achieve Equal Representation of Minority Students*. Washington, D.C.: U.S. Government Printing Office.

Heiss, Jerold, 1975. *The Case of the Black Family*. New York: Columbia University Press.

Hoffer, Eric. 1963. *The Ordeal of Changes*. New York: Harper and Row.

Holden, Matthew, Jr. 1958a. *County Government in Ohio*. Cleveland: Metropolitan Service Commission.

_____. 1958b. *Intergovernmental Agreements in the Cleveland Metropolitan Area*. Cleveland: Cleveland Metropolitan Service Commission.

_____. 1963. "Litigation and the Political Order." *Western Political Quarterly* 16 (December): 771–781.

_____. 1966. *Pollution Control as a Bargaining Process: An Essay on Regulatory Decision-Making*. Ithaca: Cornell University Water Resource Center.

_____. 1968. "On the Misunderstanding of Important Phenomena." *Urban Affairs Quarterly* (September).

_____. 1971. "Black Politicians in the Time of the 'New' Urban Politics." *The Review of Black Political Economy* 2, No. 1.

_____. Dresang, L. 1975. *What Government Does*, Beverly Hills: Sage Publications.

_____. 1973. "Judgement and the Right Questions." *American Politics Quarterly* (April).

Jencks, Christopher, et al. 1972. *Inequality.* New York: Basic Books.

Jencks, Christopher, and Riesman, David. 1967. "The American Negro College." *Harvard Educational Review* 37 (Winter): 3–60.

Jones, Mary Cover. 1960. "The Later Careers of Boys Who were Early or Late-Maturing." In J. M. Seidman, ed., *The Adolescent.* New York: Holt, Rinehart, and Winston, pp. 804–822.

Kannerstein, Gregory. 1978. "Black Colleges: Self-Concept." In Charles V. Willie and Ronald R. Edmonds, eds., *Black Colleges in America.* New York: Teachers College Press, pp. 29–50.

Kriesberg, Louis. 1968. "Intergenerational Patterns of Poverty." Paper presented at the Annual Meeting of the Eastern Sociological Society, Boston, April 6.

Landes, David S., and Tilly, Charles, eds., 1971. *History as Social Science.* Englewood Cliffs, N.J.: Prentice-Hall.

Lehman, Harvey C. 1946. "The Age of Starting to Contribute Versus Total Creative Output." *Journal of Applied Psychology* 30: 460–468.

_____. 1947. "The Age of Eminent Leaders: Then and Now," *American Journal of Sociology* 52: 342–350.

Levinson, Daniel J. 1978. *The Season's of a Man's Life.* New York: Ballantine Books.

Lewis, W. Arthur. 1954. *Economic Problems of Today.*

_____. 1955. *The Theory of Economic Growth.* Homewood, Ill.: Richard I. Irwin.

_____. 1966a. *Development Planning.* London: George Allen.

_____. 1966b. *The Politics of Africa.*

_____. 1967. *Reflections on Nigeria's Economic Growth.* Paris: Development Centre of the Organization for Economic Cooperation and Development.

_____. 1969a. *Some Aspects of Economic Development.*

_____. 1969b. *Aspects of Tropical Trade, 1883–1965.*

Leiberson, Stanley, and Carter, Donna K. 1979. "Making It in America: Differences Between Eminent Black and White Ethnic Groups." *American Sociological Review* 44 (June): 347–366.

Merton, Robert K. 1968. *Social Theory and Social Structure.* New York: Free Press.

Mitchell, G. Duncan. 1968. *A Hundred Years of Sociology.* Chicago: Aldine.

Monro, John. 1978. "Teaching and Learning English." In Charles V. Willie and Ronald R. Edmonds, eds., *Black Colleges in America.* New York: Teachers College Press, pp. 235–260.

Moore, Harry T. 1971. "Preface." In Darwin T. Turner, *In a Minor Chord.* Carbondale: Southern Illinois University Press, pp. vii–xi.

Nagel, Stuart S. 1975. "Series Editor's Introduction." In Matthew Holden, Jr. and Dennis L. Dresang, eds., *What Government Does.* Beverly Hills, Calif.: Sage Publications.

National Advisory Committee on Black Higher Education and Black Colleges and Universities. 1979. *Access of Black Americans to Higher Education: How Open Is the Door?* Washington, D.C.: U.S. Government Printing Office.

National Center for Education Statistics. 1980. *Digest of Education Statistics.* Washington, D.C.: U.S. Government Printing Office.

Newman, Dorothy K.; Amidei, Nancy J.; Carter, Barbara L.; Day, Dawn; Kruvant, William J., and Russell, Jack S. 1978. *Protest, Politics and Prosperity*. New York: Pantheon Books.

Odegaard, Charles E. 1977. *Minorities in Medicine*. New York: the Josiah Macy, Jr. Foundation.

Peirce, Neal R. 1981. "The'NIMBY' Syndrome." *Boston Globe*, September 28, p. 14.

Phi Delta Kappan, Inc. 1978. "The Tenth Annual Gallup Poll of the Public Attitudes Toward the Public School." *Phi Delta Kappan* (September).

Rawls, John. 1971. *A Theory of Justice*. Cambridge, Mass.: Harvard University Press.

Riesman, David, and Jencks, Christopher. 1968. *The Academic Revolution*. New York: Doubleday.

Rosenblatt, Roger. 1974. *Black Fiction*. Cambridge, Mass.: Harvard University Press.

Smith, Charles U. 1976. "Teaching and Learning the Social Sciences in the Predominantly Black Universities." In C. V. Willie and R. R. Edmonds, eds., *Black Colleges in America*. New York: Teachers College Press.

Smith, Huston. 1976. *Forgotten Truth*. New York: Harper.

Solmon, Lewis, and Taubman, Paul J. 1973. *Does College Matter?* New York: Academic Press.

Sanley, Manfred. 1978. *The Technnological Conscience*. New York: Free Press.

Star, Jack. 1977. "Above All, A Scholar." *Change* (February): 27–33.

Stonequist, Everett B. 1937. *The Marginal Man*. New York: Scribner's.

Stouffer, Samuel A. 1980. *An Experimental Comparison of Statistical and History Methods of Attitude Research*. New York: Arno Press. (Presented dissertation at the University of Chicago in 1930.)

Taylor, Howard F. 1977. "Playing the Dozens with Path Analysis." In Raymond L. Hall, ed., *Black Separatism and Social Reality: Rhetoric and Reason*. New York: Pergamon, pp. 243–250.

Terman, Lewis, and Oden, Melita. 1947. *The Gifted Child Grows Up*. Stanford: Stanford University Press.

_____. 1960. "The Gifted Group at Mid-Life: Fulfillment of Promise." In Jerome M. Seidman, ed., *The Adolescent—A Book of Readings, rev. ed.* New York: Holt, Rinehart and Winston, pp. 823–833. (Originally published, 1953.)

Thompson, Daniel C. 1973. *Private Black Colleges at the Crossroads*. Westport, Conn.: Greenwood Press.

Tribble, Israel, Jr. 1979. "A Black Perspective on 'The Case Against' College." *Educational Forum* (May):421–427.

Turner, Darwin T. 1964. *Katharsis*. Wellesley: Wellesley Press.

Turner, Darwin T. 1965. *Images of the Negro in America*. Boston, D. C. Heath.

_____. 1967. *Nathaniel Hawthorne's "The Scarlet Letter."*

_____. 1968. "The Negro Dramatist's Image of the Universe." Abraham Chapman, ed., *Black Voices*. New York: Mentor Books, p. 677–699.

_____. 1969. *Black American Literature: Essays*. Columbus: Charles Merrill.

_____. 1969. *Black American Literature: Fiction*. Columbus: Charles Merrill.

_____. 1969. *Black American Literature: Poetry*. Columbus: Charles Merrill.

_____. 1970. *Black American Literature: Essays, Poetry, Fiction, Drama*. Columbus: Charles Merrill.

_____. 1969. "Introduction." In *The House Behind the Cedars* by Charles W. Chestnut. New York: Collier Books. (Originally published, 1900.)

_____. 1970. *Black American Literature: Essays, Poetry, Fiction, Drama.* Columbus, Ohio: Charles Merrill.

_____. 1971a. *In a Minor Chord.* Carbondale, Ill: Southern Illinois University Press.

_____. 1971b. *Black Drama in America: An Anthology.* Greenwich, Fawcett.

_____. et al. 1972a. *Voices From the Black Experience: African and Afro-American Literature.* Boston: Ginn.

_____. 1972b. *The Teaching of Literature by Afro-American Writers: theory and practice.* National Council of Teacher of English.

U.S. Bureau of the Census. 1960. *Statistical Abstract of the United States:* Washington, D.C.: U.S. Government Printing Office.

_____. 1979. *Statistical Abstract of the United States: 1979.* Washington, D.C.: U.S. Government Printing Office.

_____. 1980. *Social Indicators III.* Washington, D.C.: U.S. Government Printing Office.

U.S. Civil Rights Commission. 1978. *Social Indicators of Equality for Minorities and Women.* Washington, D.C.: U.S. Government Printing Office.

Wharton, Clifton R., Jr. 1972. "Reflections on Black Intellectual Power." *Educational Record* (Fall):281–282.

Willie, Charles V. 1979. *The Caste and Class Controversy.* Bayside, N.Y.: General Hall.

_____. 1979. "The Relative Effects of Race and Social Class on Family Income." C. V. Willie, ed., *The Caste and Class Controversy.* Bayside, N.Y.: General Hall, pp. 60–61.

_____. 1980. *Leadership Development for Minorities.* New York: Rockefeller Foundation.

_____. 1981. *The Ivory and Ebony Towers.* Lexington, Mass.: Lexington Books.

_____. and Edmonds, Ronald R. 1978. *Black Colleges in America.* New York: Teachers College Press.

_____. and MacLeish, Marlene. 1978. "The Priorities of presidents of Black Colleges." In Charles V. Willie and Ronald R. Edmonds, eds., *Black Colleges in America.* New York: Teachers College press.

Wilson, William, Julius. 1978. *The Declining Significance of Race.* Chicago: University of Chicago Press.

_____. 1979. "The Declining Significance of Race, Revisited but Not Revised." In C. V. Willie, ed., *The Caste and Class Controversy.* Bayside, N.Y.: General Hall, p. 166.

Wright, Richard, and Rosskam, G. 1941. *12 Million Black Voices.* New York: Viking.

Index

A

action, compensatory
  and career stage, 99–100
  and family stage, 104–105
action, social, and social
    psychology
  Kenneth B. Clark, 44
action elements, 7
administration. *See also*
    public policy
  John Hope Franklin, 14,
    22–26
  and scholarship, 100–101
  Darwin T. Turner, 77,
    82–84
Africa
  W. Arthur Lewis, 34–35
American Council of
    Learned Societies
  Darwin T. Turner, 86
American Economic
    Association, 2
  W. Arthur Lewis, 35–36,
    39
American Economic Review
  W. Arthur Lewis, 30

American Historical
    Association, 2
  John Hope Franklin, 23
American Psychological
    Association, 2
  Kenneth B. Clark, 45, 55
American Political Science
    Association, 2
  Matthew Holden, Jr., 61,
    69
*American Political Science
    Review*
  Matthew Holden, Jr., 69
American Society of Public
    Administration,
    Wisconsin Capital
    Chapter
  Matthew Holden, Jr., 69
American Studies
    Association
  John Hope Franklin, 23
anthropology
  Matthew Holden, Jr., 68
Aristotle
  Matthew Holden, Jr., 69
Asia
  John Hope Franklin, 24

LIBRARY
ST. LOUIS COMMUNITY COLLEGE
AT FLORISSANT VALLEY